ANIMAL GUIDANCE

Sharon Brown

Copyright © 2023 by Sharon Brown

All rights reserved. No part of this publication may be reproduced, distributed or transmitted in any form or by any means without permission of the publisher, except in the case of brief quotations referencing the body of work and in accordance with copyright law.

The information given in this book should not be treated as a substitute for professional medical advice; always consult a medical practitioner. Any use of information in this book is at the reader's discretion and risk. Neither the author nor the publisher can be held responsible for any loss, claim or damage arising out of the use, or misuse, of the suggestions made, the failure to take medical advice or for any material on third party websites.

ISBN:

978-1-913590-75-8 (Hardback)
978-1-913590-76-5 (ebook)

Cover design by Lynda Mangoro
Illustrations by Jennifer Parris

The Unbound Press
www.theunboundpress.com

Hey unbound one!

Welcome to this magical book brought to you by The Unbound Press.

At The Unbound Press, we believe that when women write freely from the fullest expression of who they are, it can't help but activate a feeling of deep connection and transformation in others. When we come together, we become more and we're changing the world, one book at a time!

This book has been carefully crafted by both the author and publisher with the intention of inspiring you to move ever more deeply into who you truly are.

We hope that this book helps you to connect with your Unbound Self and that you feel called to pass it on to others who want to live a more fully expressed life.

With much love,

Nicola Humber

Founder of The Unbound Press
www.theunboundpress.com

Dedication

To my husband, Bernard, and my two sons, Eirnín and Ciarán. No matter how mad they thought I was (am), they still encouraged me to follow my dreams.

Dreams do come true; you just need belief and trust, and a little bit of pixie dust.

Contents

How I First Started Connecting with the Animal Guides ... 11
How This Book Was Birthed ... 13
Connecting with your Animal Guides ... 15
How to Use This Book ... 19

DAILY GUIDANCE

1. ELEPHANT – Obstacles ... 23
2. DRAGONFLY – Magic ... 24
3. HORSE – Freedom ... 25
4. DEER – Let Go ... 26
5. EAGLE – Mastery ... 27
6. LION – Strength and Courage ... 28
7. MONKEY – Monkey Mind ... 29
8. DOG – Pause ... 30
9. CAT – Independence ... 31
10. OWL – InnerVision ... 32
11. HUMMINGBIRD – Miracles ... 33
12. SQUIRREL – Distraction ... 34
13. BEAR – Power ... 35
14. BEE – Abundance ... 36
15. MOUSE – Movement ... 37
16. RABBIT – Recentre ... 38
17. SPIDER – Web of Life ... 39
18. FOX – Confrontation ... 40
19. WHITE STAG – Old Wisdom ... 41
20. WOLF – Instinct ... 42
21. COW – Moo-dy ... 43
22. SHEEP – Simplify ... 44
23. BADGER – Mask ... 45
24. ROBIN – Messenger ... 46
25. BLACKBIRD – Mystical ... 47
26. WEASEL – Dedication ... 48
27. BUFFALO – Assistance ... 49
28. TIGER – Unstoppable ... 50
29. RHINO – Fear ... 51
30. LADYBIRD – Luck ... 52
31. HAMSTER – Fun ... 53
32. RAT – Dedication ... 54
33. PIG – Opportunities ... 55
34. HEN – Curiosity ... 56
35. PEACOCK – Confidence ... 57
36. DOLPHIN – Inner Child ... 58
37. SHARK – Bitten Off ... 59
38. WHALE – Emotions ... 60
39. OCTOPUS – Drive ... 61
40. SEAHORSE – Flow ... 62
41. GOAT – Guilt ... 63
42. SNAKE – Transformation ... 64
43. GORILLA – Vulnerability ... 65
44. CAMEL – Nurture ... 66
45. GIRAFFE – Unique ... 67
46. LEOPARD – Old Issues ... 68
47. PANDA – Black and White ... 69
48. WORM – Grounding ... 70
49. HIPPO – Questioning Oneself ... 71
50. PARROT – Experience ... 72
51. MEERKAT – Awareness ... 73
52. PANDA – Gentle ... 74
53. ZEBRA – Recognition ... 75
54. HEDGEHOG – Compliance ... 76

#	Entry	Page
55.	POLAR BEAR – Endurance	77
56.	SEA LION – Ability	78
57.	ANTELOPE – Energy	79
58.	CHAMELEON – Guide	80
59.	SLOTH – Patience	81
60.	DUCK – Comfort	82
61.	DONKEY – Challenges	83
62.	CRAB – Holding On	84
63.	WASP – Held Back	85
64.	FLY – Listening	86
65.	BUTTERFLY – Transcend	87
66.	PENGUIN – Teamwork	88
67.	OSTRICH – Burying	89
68.	CROCODILE – Hard Exterior	90
69.	EMU – Excellence	91
70.	KANGAROO – NewPath	92
71.	KOALA BEAR – Take it Easy	93
72.	PORCUPINE – Chaos	94
73.	COYOTE – Guide	95
74.	RACOON – Problem Solved	96
75.	CHEETAH – Speed	97
76.	JAGUAR – InnerPower	98
77.	LYNX – Moon Energy	99
78.	OTTER – Joy	100
79.	MOOSE – Pride	101
80.	ELK – Rut	102
81.	HOG – NewLife	103
82.	LIZARD – Cycles	104
83.	SCORPION – Self-Protection	105
84.	GOLDFISH – Prosperity	106
85.	WOMBAT – Foundation	107
86.	CHIPMUNK – Restless	108
87.	POSSUM – LayLow	109
88.	HYENA – StrongWilled	110
89.	CHIMPANZEE – Committed	111
90.	JELLYFISH – Faith	112
91.	BAT – Shadow Side	113
92.	HARE – Femininity	114
93.	FROG – Hop to it	115
94.	MOLE – Fresh Air	116
95.	ANT – Willpower	117
96.	BEETLE – Diet	118
97.	TORTOISE – Easy does it	119
98.	SNAIL – Stress	120
99.	SWAN – Soulmate	121
100.	WOODPECKER – Family Life	122
101.	SALMON – Movement	123
102.	LIONESS – Carefree	124
103.	BEAGLE – God	125
104.	CAT – Standing in Your Power	126
105.	STALLION – Fenced In	127
106.	FIELD MOUSE – Low Self-Esteem	128
107.	WHITE RABBIT – Stop Hiding!	129
108.	SPIDER – Detail	130
109.	ARCTIC FOX – Tricky Situation	131
110.	RED STAG – Masculine Side	132
111.	WOLF – Support from Your Pack	133
112.	CROW – Life's Magic	134
113.	COW – Generosity	135
114.	SHEEP – Unworthy	136
115.	BADGER – Walk Your Own Path	137
116.	ROBIN – Christ Consciousness Energy	138
117.	EAGLE – Time to Take Flight	139
118.	BLACKBIRD – Mediumship/ Clairvoyant	140
119.	WEASEL – Silence	141
120.	WHITE BUFFALO – ChoosePeace	142
121.	ELEPHANT – Goddess	143
122.	INDIAN TIGER – Inner Warrior	144
123.	WHITE RHINO – Stability	145
124.	LADYBIRD – Dare	146
125.	HAMSTER – Round and Round	147
126.	RAT – BigThings	148
127.	PIG – Sniffing	149
128.	HEN – Time	150
129.	PEACOCK – Third Eye	151
130.	DOLPHIN – Manifest	152
131.	WHALE – Bridge the Gap	153
132.	SHARK – Environment	154
133.	OCTOPUS – Creativity	155
134.	SEA HORSE – Inspire	156

135. GOAT – Seeing the World	157	
136. SNAKE – Kundalini	158	
137. MONKEY – See!	159	
138. GORILLA – Vocalise	160	
139. DEER – See Yourself	161	
140. CAMEL – Hydration	162	
141. GIRAFFE – Visualisation	163	
142. LEOPARD – Motivation	164	
143. PANDA – Balance	165	
144. WORM – Healing Insecureties	166	
145. HIPPO – Suppressed	167	
146. PARROT – Ask for Help	168	
147. MEERKAT – Anger	169	
148. PANDA – Honour Yourself	170	
149. ZEBRA – Compromise	171	
150. HEDGEHOG – Unleash Yourself	172	
151. OWL – End of a Cycle	173	
152. BEAR – Leadership	174	
153. POLAR BEAR – Quiet Time	175	
154. SEA LION – Focus	176	
155. ANTELOPE – Happening Quickly	177	
156. CHAMELEON – Blending into the Background	178	
157. SLOTH – Carefree	179	
158. DUCK – Reconnection	180	
159. DONKEY – DeepTruth	181	
160. CRAB – New Direction	182	
161. BEE – Hard Working	183	
162. WASP – Development	184	
163. FLY – Persistent	185	
164. BUTTERFLY – Take your Time	186	
165. PENGUIN – Chaos	187	
166. OSTRICH – Declutter	188	
167. CROCODILE – Forceful	189	
168. EMU – Excellence	190	
169. KANGAROO – Leap of Faith	191	
170. KOALA BEAR – Mindful	192	
171. PORCUPINE – Head On	193	
172. COYOTE – Trickster	194	
173. RACCOON – Secrecy	195	
174. CHEETAH – Procrastination	196	
175. JAGUAR - Gatekeeper	197	
176. LYNX – Promise	198	
177. OTTER – Unite	199	
178. MOOSE – Temporary	200	
179. ELK – It's OK to Say No	201	
180. HOG – Sociable	202	
181. LIZARD – Messenger	203	
182. SCORPION – Egypt	204	
183. GOLDFISH – Bowl	205	
184. WOMBAT – Aggressive	206	
185. CHIPMUNK – Adventurers	207	
186. POSSUM – Underestimated	208	
187. HYENA – Community	209	
188. CHIMPANZEE – Understanding Oneself	210	
189. JELLYFISH – The Power of Intention	211	
190. SQUIRREL – Last Minute	212	
191. BAT – Misunderstood	213	
192. HARE – Ancestral Healing	214	
193. FROG – Education	215	
194. MOLE – True/False	216	
195. ANT – Effort	217	
196. BEETLE – Insignificant	218	
197. DRAGONFLY – DeepThought	219	
198. HUMMINGBIRD – Little Pleasures	220	
199. TORTOISE – Harmony	221	
200. SNAIL – What is Your Hurry?	222	
201. BLACK SWAN - Making the Impossible Possible	223	
202. WOODPECKER – Never One to Give Up	224	
203. SALMON –Living Life to the Fullest	225	
204. DOG – Selfless	226	
205. CAT – Quirky	227	
206. HORSE – Appetite forLife	228	
207. MOUSE – What You Missed?	229	
208. RABBIT – Spontaneity	230	
209. SPIDER – Entangled	231	
210. FOX – Swift	232	
211. STAG – Regeneration	233	
212. WOLF –Lack of Trust	234	
213. CROW –Walk Your Talk	235	
214.BULL – Stand Your Ground	236	

215. RAM – Defiant Attitude	237
216. BADGER – InnerVoice	238
217. ROBIN – Decluttering	239
218. EAGLE – Hope	240
219. BLACKBIRD – Culture	241
220. WEASEL – Self-Judgement	242
221. BUFFALO – Brave Face	243
222. ELEPHANT – Commitment	244
223. LIONESS – Command	245
224. WHITE TIGER – War	246
225. WHALE – Watch YourWords	247
226. LADYBIRD – Invest	248
227. HAMSTER – EnjoyYour Achievements	249
228. RAT – Shrewd	250
229. PIG – Mysteries	251
230. HEN – Sharp	252
231. PEACOCK – Beauty	253
232. DOLPHIN – Resurrection	254
233. WHALE – Importance of Community	255
234. SHARK – Authority	256
235. OCTOPUS – Master of Disguise	257
236. SEAHORSE – Contented	258
237. MOUNTAIN GOAT – Valuable Lesson	259
238. SNAKE – Primal Energy	260
239. MONKEY – Explore	261
240. SILVERBACK GORILLA – Dignified	262
241. FAWN – Innocence	263
242. CAMEL – Close to Your Chest	264
243. GIRAFFE – Entangled	265
244. LEOPARD – Simplicity	266
245. RED PANDA – Tree Wisdom	267
246. WORM – Dig Deep	268
247. HIPPO – Calmness	269
248. PARROT – Wonder	270
249. MEERKAT – Quick-Witted	271
250. PANDA – Heart Walls	272
251. ZEBRA – Timeout	273
252. HEDGEHOG – Natural Curiosity	274
253. OWL – Presence	275
254. BEAR – WiseTeacher	276
255. POLAR BEAR – A Test inTime	277
256. SEA LION – Clues	278
257. ANTELOPE – Happening Quickly	279
258. CHAMELEON – Eyes on thePrize	280
259. SLOTH – BePresent	281
260. DUCK – Insignificant	282
261. DONKEY – Don't Waver	283
262. CRAB – A Different Approach	284
263. BEE – Deviation	285
264. WASP – Caution	286
265. FLY – A Keen Eye	287
266. BUTTERFLY – Navigate	288
267. PENGUIN – Endure Suffering	289
268. OSTRICH – Limitation	290
269. CROCODILE – Thick-Skinned	291
270. EMU – Victimisation	292
271. KANGAROO – Dreams	293
272. KOALA BEAR – Appearances	294
273. PORCUPINE – Face Your Vulnerabilities	295
274. COYOTE – Fooled Once	296
275. RACOON – Calm Under Pressure	297
276. CHEETAH – Too Many Goals	298
277. JAGUAR – Cut Through the Bullshit	299
278. LYNX – Paying Attention	300
279. OTTER – What If?	301
280. MOOSE – Native American Guide	302
281. ELK – Pace Yourself	303
282. HOG – Stop Waiting	304
283. LIZARD – What is Your Heart Telling You?	305
284. SCORPION – Upper Hand	306
285. GOLDFISH – Pushing Against the Current	307
286. WOMBAT – Wise Advice	308
287. CHIPMUNK – Always Planning Ahead	309
288. POSSUM – Environment	310
289. HYENA – Be Light of Heart	311
290. CHIMPANZEE – Act Fast	312
291. JELLYFISH – Take Everything in Stride	313
292. SQUIRREL – Better Days Ahead	314
293. BAT – Deep-Rooted Fears	315
294. HARE – Spring Clean	316

295. FROG – Cleansing Through Water	317
296. MOLE – Connecting with Earth's Rhythm	318
297. ANT – Organised	319
298. BEETLE –Take Responsibility	320
299. DRAGONFLY – Habits That Need to Change	321
300. HUMMINGBIRD – Seek Guidance	322
301. TORTOISE – Carrying Too Much	323
302. SNAIL – Use Your Time Wisely	324
303. SWAN – Upper Limits	325
304. WOODPECKER – Door OpenWide	326
305. SALMON – Travel	327
306. CROW – Powerful Foresight	328
307. DOG – Sociable	329
308. CAT – Reassurance	330
309. HORSE – Competitive	331
310. MOUSE – Stay onTrack	332
311. RABBIT – Lucky Charm	333
312. SPIDER – ClearPath	334
313. FOX – Sense of Humour	335
314. WHITE STAG – Air Element	336
315. WOLF – Make Your Position Known	337
316. COW – Relish Stability	338
317. BLACK SHEEP – Sheeple	339
318. BADGER – Seek Solitude	340
319. ROBIN – Turning a Blind Eye	341
320. EAGLE – Personal Freedom	342
321. BLACKBIRD – Values	343
322. WEASEL – Intervention	344
323. BUFFALO – Stay True to Yourself	345
324. ELEPHANT – Seek Harmony	346
325. LION – Let Your Wild Side Out	347
326. TIGER – Rash Decisions	348
327. RHINO – Seeing Lack	349
328. LADYBIRD – Remedies	350
329. HAMSTER – Be Mindful of Your Health	351
330. RAT – Uncertain Steps Forward	352
331. PIG – You Deserve it	353
332. HEN – Explore Further	354
333. PEACOCK – Pride	355
334. DOLPHIN – Element of Water	356
335. WHALE – Find Your True Voice	357
336. SHARK – Full Potential	358
337. OCTOPUS – Open Mind	359
338. SEAHORSE – Charm	360
339. GOAT – Sacrificed	361
340. SNAKE – A Fresh Start	362
341. MONKEY – Trickster	363
342. Gorilla – Overreact	364
343. DEER – Hectic Life	365
344. CAMEL – Restore and Replenish	366
345. GIRAFFE – Expressing Your Individuality with Pride	367
346. SNOW LEOPARD – Good Karma	368
347. PANDA – Integrate	369
348. WORM – DiscoverYourReal Strengths	370
349. HIPPO – Stagnation	371
350. PARROT – Colours	372
351. MEERKAT – Gossip	373
352. PANTHER – Elusive	374
353. ZEBRA – Thinking on Your Feet	375
354. HEDGEHOG – Emerging Victorious	376
355. OWL – Graduation	377
356. BEAR – Feng Shui	378
357. POLAR BEAR – Emotional Baggage	379
358. SEA LION – Opportunity Passing You By	380
359. ANTELOPE – Knowing Yourself	381
360. CHAMELEON – Environment	382
361. SLOTH – Avoidance	383
362. DUCK – Be Ready, Be Prepared	384
363. DONKEY – Extremely Cautious	385
364. CRAB – Sideways	386
365. BEE –Trust in the Miracles	387
Acknowledgments	388
About the Author	390
About the Artist	391

How I First Started Connecting with the Animal Guides

It was November 2015, and I was on a retreat with my then mentor, Aishling Mooney (who was my first spiritual mentor). We were in a beautiful space in Dublin. There was me, Aishling and two others. It was on a Saturday afternoon, and Aishling asked us all to demonstrate to each other our gifts. Deidre went first, using symbols and explaining her work as a play therapist. Then Niamh explained what she did; I was totally blown away by these two amazing ladies; all the way through it, I was saying to myself, 'I can only heal people; I just do Reiki.' I was in total overwhelm.

It came to my turn, and, OMG, I felt sick. Aishling said to share my gifts, and I said I could only do reiki; I felt so nervous and useless. Then Aishling said, 'Sharon, you know how much you love animals?' I said yes, not knowing where this was going. Then Aishling said to me, 'Take a deep breath in and just relax,' so I did. She said, 'What animal do you see?' Then in front of my eyes, I saw Aishling shapeshift into a beautiful butterfly; I thought I was losing my mind. I told her what I saw, and then Aishling said to me, cool as you like, 'Ok, what is the message the butterfly has for me?' I just allowed the butterfly to speak through me and gave the message. I was completely blown away by what had just happened. Then Aishling asked me to do it for Deirdre and Niamh, so I did. Deirdre shapeshifted into a gorgeous brown bear, so I trusted and gave the message. Then Niamh shapeshifted into a stunning peacock; so again, I trusted and gave the message. I was totally on a high and just could not believe what had happened.

On my way home, I rang a friend to tell her about the experience. When I was telling her, I did feel it was a bit woohoo; she was delighted for me. I got home and was telling my family how I got on, but I left out the animal guides as I just didn't feel ready to say it out loud. I was sitting down for dinner with my husband and two boys, and as I looked up at Bernard, he started to shapeshift into his animal guide, a giraffe. Then I looked at my eldest son, and he shapeshifted into a koala, and my youngest son shapeshifted into a penguin. Needless to say, I nearly choked on my dinner. I just started laughing, as I hadn't planned on saying anything to my family about what had happened with the animal guides earlier that day. But the animal guides wanted to be seen and spoken about, so I told them what I was seeing. We had a good laugh about it, but they did look at me as if I was mad – they still do at times.

It did take me a good long while to fully embrace them. I used to try to ignore them, but they won't let up. After a while, they started coming into my healings, and I would shapeshift into different animals and use their essence in my healing. They also started to give me healing codes, which I still use today in my work.

They have shown me how to have fun, laugh, and really go for my dreams. You have to have a sense of humour when working with the animal guides. At times over the years, I have had a spiritual zoo in my home. I would often say to myself, *If only others could see what I see, and see the madness and fun.* They have helped me embrace who I am today.

How This Book Was Birthed

For many years, I have been connecting with the animal guides on a daily basis; I call them all the time for different things. Then out of the blue, I got the guidance from them, *You need to write a book*. I said to myself, *No hope; how would I be able to write a book? This has to be my ego*. I had a good laugh with myself and thought it was a great joke. The joke is on me.

Then at least once a week, I was getting the same thing over and over again, *book, book, book*. I didn't want to hear it or do it. I didn't have confidence in myself. I told a close friend of mine, and she said to me, 'Wow, great idea, just go for it!' I did sit with it for a while – I was hoping it would go away.

One day during the summer, I was sitting out, enjoying the sun, and I picked up my journal and said to myself, 'Ok, here goes …' With that, I could feel all the animal guides gathering around me. My own wolf guide said to me, 'It's about time. I never thought you were going to start; better late than never.' From there on, each day when I had a minute, I would sit in the garden armed with pen and paper, and I allowed each message to come in. They were lining up in front of me – they all wanted their say.

I got to 101 messages, and I thought I was finished. But then I got more guidance – there were to be 365 messages, one for each day of the year. Of course, I tried to ignore it and dismiss it, like I do all the time. But no, they wouldn't allow it. There were times when I was channelling this book that I felt like I had a spiritual zoo in my home, as I said before, and it felt magical having the animal guides all around me. They show me the funniest things at times, and they always keep me grounded. So, I gave in and kept writing until I had my 365 messages.

'You'll notice that some of the animals show up at different times with different messages. Just like humans, some animals just have more to say! So when some of the animals kept coming back with different messages, I decided to include them all.

I know the book had to be illustrated, and the first person that popped into my head was a client and friend, Jenny Parris. I met Jenny when I was working with my mentor Aishling Mooney, many years ago; I connected Jenny with her animal guide, Elvis. Elvis is a snake. Jenny worked with me 1-2-1. Basically, I always knew that she had to do art for me, but at that time, I wasn't called to ask her to do a painting for me – now I know why. I connected with Jenny to ask her to do the illustrations for the book, and she was delighted. I only had the first half of the book done at this time, so I continued to channel the rest as Jenny started the illustrations.

When Jenny sent me the first one, I got this overwhelming feeling, like, *This is real, it's really happening, no turning back now*! Each week, I looked forward to receiving the illustrations Jenny created. As you will see in this book, Jenny did an amazing job – she brought the spirit of each animal alive in each drawing.

I hope you enjoy this book as much as I enjoyed creating it.

Love and blessings,

Sharon and the animal guides xx

Connecting with your Animal Guides

Over the past couple of years, I have built up a connection with Animal guides. For anyone who is unaware of what an animal guide is, it is a guide in the form of an animal who can help you in any aspect of your life. Animal guides can be used on a daily basis the same way you use your angels and archangels.

There is an animal guide there to help everyone. You just need to call them in and use their energy to help you, no matter what is going on in your life. They are only too willing to help, but they cannot help unless you ask. Your animal guide can change and adapt to suit the situation that you are in, but you will more than likely always have your main animal guide around you anyway.

I have always had a pure love for animals. Personally, I have two wolf animal guides. Their names are Rodger and Dodger. One is for protection, and the other is for spiritual knowledge. I use their assistance in every aspect of my life, but I also have many other animal guides to assist me on a daily basis. So now I am going to explain to you how you can do this for yourself and get your own animal guide involved in your life and begin this beautiful journey.

I am going to show you a simple and easy technique to help you start to connect with your animal guide for yourself.

1. Light a candle.
2. Ground yourself by visualising two golden roots coming from your feet going into the ground and into the core of Mother Earth.
3. Close your eyes, and whatever animal presents itself to you is your animal guide.
4. Ask them their name.

5. You will then receive the guidance that you need.

6. The only thing that you need to do at this time is to trust and write down the information that you receive for future reference.

7. Don't lose heart if you don't get a name for your animal guide on your first attempt. You may not be ready to receive the information, and you just have to build up trust between you and your animal guide.

Another way to receive information and messages from your animal guide is to try the following automatic writing exercise. All you need is a piece of paper, pen, and a candle (the candle is not necessary – do what feels right for you).

8. Light the candle.

9. Ground yourself by visualising two golden roots coming from your feet going into the ground and into the core of Mother Earth.

10. Call in the energy of the animal guide you want to connect with.

11. Sit and feel their energy around you.

12. Write the first thing that comes into your head (this is the information from your guide).

13. Don't force it to happen, just write. Don't overthink it – go with the flow.

14. Trust and believe in the information you are receiving.

Next, I am going to share with you another little secret on how to feel the energy and presence of your animal guides around you.

15. Light a candle.

16. Ground yourself by visualising two golden roots coming from your feet going into the ground and into the core of Mother Earth.

17. Call in the energy of the animal guide you want to connect with.

18. Ask them to stand behind you. You may feel cold or hot energy. Close your eyes – you may see them with your third eye, but don't worry if you don't.

19. Ask them to place their paw or wing on your shoulder.

20. Don't second-guess this, as you will feel their presence.

21. Enjoy the experience.

You can also use your animal guides in every part of your life. For example, you can call in the wolf for protection. You could call in the dolphin to bring happiness and fun and childlike wonder into your life. Call in the bear for strength and courage, or the owl for wisdom. Animal guides have many messages and guidance for people, and they need the world to be aware of their existence and power as they have insight and guidance to share with everyone.

My role, as given to me by the animal guide realm, is to be their voice for the world to hear. They have guided and trusted me to create many online courses, including 'Spirit Animal Transformational Healing', 'Golden Web of Abundance with the Spider', 'Chakra Clearing Using Spirit Animal Wisdom', 'Celtic Animal Zodiacs', 'Soul Alignment Programme', 'Self-Embodiment', and 'Daring to Be U with the Spirit Animal Guidance of the Lion'. I have also been blessed with the ability to give animal guidance readings. So, as you can see, they have helped me in many different areas of my life and business so that I can help others along their own personal journey.

Their mission is for the world to hear the voice of the animal guide kingdom as they have guidance for each and every one of us. Their theme is to DREAM BIG. Bring the love, the joy, the fun, and the laughter back into people's lives as this will bring them back to their soul life purpose and realign them to their biggest dreams.

I wish you all a fantastic journey connecting with your animal guides.

I am now going to share with you all a message that was channelled to me from my very special animal guides.

Message from My Animal Guides, Roger and Dodger:

There are a lot of animal guides waiting for you to connect with them. They have so much to teach you – you just need to be open to listening to them. We cannot connect with you unless we are asked through spiritual law. So, as you can see, we can only wait for you to ask for our help and guidance. This planet is going through an awakening at this time and the old way of living does not serve you anymore. We are here to help you through this time of transition and bring you to the next level of consciousness. Don't delay – call on us. We are ready and waiting.

Lots of love and animal blessings,

Sharon Brown, Rodger, and Dodger xx

How to Use This Book

For many years now, I have been connecting with the animal guides on a daily basis. Sometimes, my personal animal guides come in, and other times it will be a random animal guide, coming in to give me guidance. Sometimes they can be a bit harsh, and I don't like what I hear or what they have to say, but they are always spot on. They don't give me fluffy, nicely-nicely messages.

I suggest that you use this book on a daily basis and add it to your morning spiritual practice. Or you can sit, ground, connect it with the book, hold it close to your chest, and ask what page number you need to open. The first number that comes into your head is the guidance you need at that moment in time.

Or you can ask what guidance you need for a specific situation; to do so, repeat the above exercise.

The best way to use this book is to trust, let go of the second-guessing, and most of all, believe in yourself – and don't forget the fun and laughter.

1. ELEPHANT – *Obstacles*

I have come here today to say, I am here to help you overcome any obstacle you may feel is holding you back. You have the strength within you to overcome this.

Yes, I know this can be hard to do. Just breathe: inhale for four seconds, hold for four, release for four, and repeat four times. Drop into your heart, and allow fear, anxiety, and overwhelm to drop away.

Now, look at the obstacle from a different place, a place of love and compassion. See the solution, take the action, and allow yourself to move forward.

You have all the wisdom you seek within you; allow it to unfold with ease and take your leadership role with love and strength.

Affirmation: *I have the strength to overcome any obstacle in my way now.*

2. DRAGONFLY – *Magic*

I have come here today to say, You have the magic within you – you just can't see it. Allow yourself to go within and unleash your magic and shine to the world.

See your reflection in the mirror and see what others see. Stop putting yourself down and see your true divine self.

What you see in others is what is in you. Look at your reflection and really see the magic you hold within.

It is time to take your rightful place in this world and allow you to fully shine and shine bright.

Affirmation: *I allow myself to see the magic within.*

3. HORSE – *Freedom*

I have come here today to ask you,

Are you feeling stuck, fed up, or maybe a bit lost? I am here to help you free yourself from this.

Sit with yourself and look at the areas in your life where you are feeling this way. See where you are holding yourself back.

When we look and see what is holding us back, we can change and set ourselves free. That discussion lies with you and only you. You are the one that can make the changes that are needed.

Take the necessary action that brings you closer to the freedom you desire; it will then set you free.

Affirmation: I am free; *I am pure love.*

4. DEER – *Let Go*

I have come here today to say, Be gentle with yourself, as you are going through a time of great healing. You are healing on all levels, mind, body, and soul.

Allow yourself to go deep within and unleash all that you are holding onto within the body. It is time to set yourself free.

Be compassionate and gentle with yourself as you go through this deep healing process. The pain, hurt, and heartache will be worth it in the end when you emerge from this with grace and pure unconditional love

See your true self-worth and step out fully into the light.

Affirmation: *I am gentle with myself; I am love.*

5. EAGLE – *Mastery*

I have come here today to say, You are the master of your own destiny; you have to believe in yourself to be the master.

Let go of all the old belief systems that you have been holding onto – they no longer serve you.

Look at what you truly want in life, make the goals, and take the action; the only one that can do it is yourself.

Self-mastery is the key to your success. Go for it, no more holding yourself back.

Affirmation: *I am the only master of my destiny*

6. LION – *Strength and Courage*

I have come here today to ask you to Hear me roar, yes, hear me roar! I am your inner strength and courage waiting to be unleashed.

It is time to unleash your truth; there is no more holding yourself back. It's time to take the steps forward – you have all that you need.

Look how far you have come. No more looking back; the only way for you is forward.

You are ready to take your rightful place on this Earth; you have the strength and courage to do this. The time for action is now.

Affirmation: *I feel great strength and courage arise in me!*

7. MONKEY – *Monkey Mind*

I have come here today to say Your mind is like a monkey jumping from branch to branch and getting nowhere. Allow yourself to concentrate on one thing at a time.

Let go of all the negative thoughts – they are doing you no good at all. Open yourself to more positive thoughts and see how life can change.

What we concentrate on, we attract; so, let go of the negative thoughts and concrete on the positive ones, and see how life can change for the better. Start believing in yourself and let go of self-judgement – nobody is perfect.

Affirmation: *I have the power to create change through positive thought now.*

8. DOG – *Pause*

I have come here today to say, It is time to stop and pause; you are at a time of reflection, a time of review, a life review. Look at how far you have come and all that you have achieved at this time.

This is a time of great contemplation. Sit back, rest, and allow the information to come in; be very clear on what you want.

When you are very clear on what you want, ask for guidance on what action you must take and then take the action.

Rest and rejuvenate until you are 100% sure about what you want; this can take time.

Affirmation: *I pause, I breathe, and I take a moment.*

9. CAT – *Independence*

I have come here today to say, You are a very independent person, and that's OK, but sometimes we need others. It is OK to ask for help; you don't always have to do it alone.

Allow yourself to ask for the help that you need. You will be surprised how you will feel when you allow yourself to receive.

Open yourself up and allow yourself to receive help. You will not be judged by others, and you will be surprised at who will come to help. We all need help from time to time; trust that the help you need is on the way.

See and allow yourself to receive and notice how sometimes life can be easier when we ask others for help.

Affirmation: *I am opening myself up to receive the help that I need now.*

10. OWL – *Inner Vision*

I have come here today to say, Choose to know the truth, because you can. Open yourself up to your inner vision. You have the ability to see the truth in everything.

The only thing that holds you back from seeing the truth is yourself. Let go of all the old patterns that hold you back, as they no longer serve you.

It is time to see the truth. You have that vision within you: unleash it and allow it to guide you through life, as it will never steer you wrong.

As you unleash the truth within you, you will rise to heights, and it will open the door to abundance in all areas of your life.

Affirmation: *I unleash my inner truth now.*

11. HUMMINGBIRD – *Miracles*

I have come here today to say, Miracles are waiting to happen. You have been asking for a miracle to happen; we have heard your prayers, and we have been working away in the background.

Have patience – this miracle is on its way. Although it might not be the way you think, it will be better than you expect, so you must not lose hope.

Trust us, and all will work out. We know it has not been easy; this is a lesson that needed to be learnt. Now is the time to think of this lesson as a blessing, open yourself up to these miracles, and receive it with gratitude.

Affirmation: *I am open to all possibilities now.*

12. SQUIRREL – *Distraction*

I have come to you today to say, Don't let life's distractions take you off course. Detach yourself from the drama around you, as this will unhinge you. Allow others to get on with their own lives. There is no need for you to interfere – this is only distracting you from what you should be doing.

What are you choosing not to look at in your own life? We always have to look within ourselves to keep on course – choose to go within instead of without.

This will help you keep yourself aligned and also to move forward to a higher vibration. When we look within ourselves, our other world changes as we are a reflection of ourselves. Choose your life, not others.

Affirmation: *I choose to focus on myself now.*

13. BEAR – *Power*

I have come to you today to say, You have the power within you to succeed in anything you do right now. You have the power to go after all your desires and dreams – the only thing stopping you is you.

Look within and see the power that you hold. Unleash it and allow yourself to expand. Go after your dreams – nobody else is going to do this for you.

It's time to make the decision and take action. Your spirit team is behind you. You cannot fail as we see the truly powerful you. This is a time of action: focus and unleash your true power.

Affirmation: *I succeed in all that I do.*

14. BEE – *Abundance*

I have come to you today to ask, What are you not seeing? Where are you not looking? Abundance is all around you – you just can't see it. You have the ability to have the abundance in life you want.

Look at the areas that you want to change; go within and release all the blocks and patterns that you are holding on to.

We hold on to old energies – ancestral, karmic, past-lives, patterns, and vows. This can affect us and the abundance we bring in. Do the inner work and release all that you hold. Allow yourself to open up to the abundance that is waiting for you. Be like the bee: allow yourself to taste the sweet nectar of life.

Affirmation: *I am open to receiving abundance in all areas of my life; this is my divine right.*

15. MOUSE – *Movement*

I have come to you today to say, This is a time of great movement for you. Sit with yourself and ask yourself where you are headed. Is it the right direction?

Ask the questions: Is this what I want? Is it my true desire? Is this aligned with my soul's path? Until you can answer these questions honestly, there is no point moving forward. You don't want to be moving in the wrong direction.

Take this time to heal and let go of the old habits that are holding you back before letting yourself move forward. Yes, there is a whole new world waiting for you, if you make the right move in the right direction.

Affirmation: *I allow myself to move forward now.*

16. RABBIT – *Recentre*

I have come to you today to ask you, Are you going down the rabbit hole?

Can you see yourself taking on outside influences or getting caught up in drama that does not belong to you?

This has become a bit of a habit for you. What are you not looking at in your life? Stop looking and getting caught up in others' drama and do your inner work to release what is holding you back. You must be 100% honest with yourself because if you don't, you are going to keep attracting this drama into your life. Stop letting others influence you and how you are feeling. You are the only one who can do this – this is an inside job. Stop and breathe; this will recentre you, and each time you feel this happen, stop, pause, breathe, and recentre.

Affirmation: *I allow myself to pause, breathe, and recentre.*

17. SPIDER – *Web of Life*

I have come to you today to ask, What webs are you weaving in your life?

Is this the life that you truly want? Are you going after your dream?

It is time to weave a new web of life. Like the Spider, we can change the direction we want to go in. You just have to believe in yourself.

Look deep within. Make the decision that you would like to change direction and go for it – there is nobody holding you back. Open yourself up to all possibilities.

Yes, you can do this. You must put your full trust in your ability to change, and know that the universe and spirit have your back. See the web of life you desire – and yes, DREAMS DO COME TRUE.

Affirmation: *I am open to infinite possibilities now.*

18. FOX – *Confrontation*

I have come to you today to say, Avoid confrontation; you have or are going to have a confrontation with someone, and this is going to upset you on a very deep level.

You need to take the higher path on this and make the first move to reconcile. It doesn't matter who was right or who was wrong; the only thing that matters is how deep this has affected you on an emotional level.

Make the first move and make contact. Tell them how you are feeling and how deeply this has hurt – they will probably feel the same as you. Forgiveness is the only way forward. You must forgive yourself and the other person so you both can move on from this. There is no point in holding on to past hurt – the only thing it gets you is dis-ease.

Affirmation: *Today, I forgive; I am free.*

19. WHITE STAG – *Old Wisdom*

I have come to you today to say, You are an old soul, an old sage.

Are you ready to unleash your old wisdom?

It is time to go within and release the true you. You have walked this Earth many times, and it is time to bring the magical wisdom to the forefront.

It is time for you to share this with the world and allow yourself to take your rightful place. You will receive the guidance that you need to allow this to happen. Trust that this is this process that you need to go through. Nobody said it was going to be easy; be gentle on yourself as you go through this.

You will feel the wisdom within you – allow it to rise and speak the tongue of the old sage. Trust that all will be OK, and you will reach new heights.

Affirmation: *I unlock my true self in divine and perfect order.*

20. WOLF – *Instinct*

I have come to you today to say, Trust your instinct; pay attention to what it is telling you. When we trust our instinct, we are never wrong. There are times when you have not trusted your instinct and you have paid the price for not trusting.

You must learn to fully trust and follow the guidance that you are getting, for it will never lead you down the wrong path.

Look at when you didn't trust and look at when you did and see how it has affected your life. When we trust in what we receive, life can be very different – it just flows. Stop second-guessing your instinct, allow new possibilities to open up, and follow your dreams.

Affirmation: *I completely trust my inner guidance.*

21. COW – *Moo-dy*

I have come to you today to ask, How are you feeling? Be honest with yourself; it's OK to feel a bit moo-dy today.

Ask yourself the questions, 'Why am I feeling this way? What or who has me feeling this way?' The only way to clear this moo-dy feeling is to acknowledge how you are feeling. See what, why, and how you are feeling this way.

When you have the answer, sit with yourself, journey on it, and let it go. If you are still feeling that way, go back and repeat the questions and go deeper; the deeper you go, the better, and the more you free yourself. Yes, it takes courage – it goes deep. Let it go and free yourself.

Affirmation: *I acknowledge how I am feeling, and I let it go.*

22. SHEEP – *Simplify*

I have come to you to ask You should look at what makes your life simple. You are taking on too much at this time and bringing yourself extra pressure.

Look at what you don't need to be doing and stop it – it's that easy. You are allowing it all to get on top of you.

Sit with yourself and write down all the things you do that are taking up your time and effort. Cross out the ones you don't need to do yourself and hand them over to someone else to do. Only concentrate on the ones you should be doing.

This will bring simplicity into your life and allow you to go through life with ease and flow.

Affirmation: *I allow my life to be simple. It's my divine right.*

23. BADGER – *Mask*

I have come to you today to ask you to Remove the mask and allow your true self to emerge.

You have different sides of yourself that you show to different people, and this is your mask. You are not allowing your true self to be seen.

Don't be afraid to allow others to see you for who you truly are. You will be surprised at the reaction that you will get.

Gather all aspects of yourself and allow yourself to be seen as one. Remove the mask and set yourself free. Free yourself. Allow your true divine self to emerge and the light that you hold within you to shine.

Affirmation: *I am allowing myself to be seen for who I truly am.*

24. ROBIN – *Messenger*

I have come to you today to say, I bring you a message from a loved one in spirit. I am with you all the time; I watch over you while you sleep. I know how much you miss me, and that's OK.

I haven't left your side since the time I passed. I know when you cry and when you are sad. I want you to know that I am OK. Stop worrying about me and live your life to the fullest. I will be with you every step of the way, guiding you from time to time.

I know you see the signs that I send you at times. I just want you to know I am by your side. When you talk to me, I can hear you. I want you to know I am with you always, and I love you.

Affirmation: *I am open to seeing the signs from spirit.*

25. BLACKBIRD – *Mystical*

I have come to you today to ask you Are you looking at the mystical side of life? Does normal not sit with you anymore? Are you looking for new, exciting ways to look at life?

I can help you unearth this within you. I will give you guidance as to what book, posts, and videos to look at.

The questions that you have been asking that have not been answered will be – I will lead you to these answers.

I will help you unleash your inner mystic that lies within. You must trust and follow the guidance I send you. Have the belief and follow the breadcrumbs that I am sending you.

Affirmation: *I trust and follow the guidance I receive.*

26. WEASEL – *Dedication*

I have come to you today to say, It's time to dedicate yourself to your goals. You have a tendency to go through life on a whim with no goals or direction in place.

Look at what you truly want in life; set out the goals that you truly want, and set the wheels in motion.

You are the only one who can do this and set yourself free. Take the necessary steps forward, even if they are baby ones – every step counts, big or small. If you don't succeed the first time, get up and try again. Rome was not built in a day – every step counts.

The key to your success is dedication and allowing yourself to succeed.

Affirmation: *I allow myself to succeed no matter what.*

27. BUFFALO – *Assistance*

I have come to you today to say, You are being asked to walk a sacred path and honour every aspect of this. You must ask the spirit realms for their help to do this and be grateful for this gift.

Also, you must connect deep with Mother Earth – this will bring you great strength. You have an important mission on the Earth and it's time to ask yourself if you're being true to this mission.

You need assistance to carry out this mission; the spirit realm is waiting to assist you on this path. You must follow the guidance with an open heart and have the strength to follow through no matter what. Your spirit team will never lead you astray. Trust and believe you are on the right path.

Affirmation: *I ask for assistance, and I receive it with gratitude.*

28. TIGER – *Unstoppable*

I have come to you today to say, You are a force to be reckoned with; you are unstoppable. Bring this energy into all areas of your life. Open yourself to new ideas that are coming in and go for it.

Feel into this energy of 'unstoppable'; see where it wants to bring you and get out of your own way. It doesn't matter if you are not sure of where it is taking you; just do it anyway, as it will work out even better than you expected.

When we allow ourselves to get out of our own way, anything is possible. This energy can make your dreams come true and bring you places you have only dreamt of – so go for it. You have nothing to lose.

Affirmation: *Dreams do come true.*

29. RHINO – *Fear*

I have come to you today to ask, Are you letting fear rule your life?

Is it taking hold of your dreams?

This is a pattern that has been going on most of your life. It is time to really look at what the fear represents. When you look at this, you will be surprised by how much it is or has affected your life.

Sit with yourself and breathe and allow all the energy of fear to surface. As it surfaces, face it head-on. Give yourself permission to release this out of your life. It is time to move forward and kick fear in the ass. Yes, you can do this. Feel it, see it, release it, and move forward. Be fearless – there is a whole new world waiting for you without fear.

Affirmation: *I move past the fear to freedom.*

30. LADYBIRD – *Luck*

I have come to you today to say, Lady Luck is on your side.

It is a great time to start a new project, set up your own business, or make the move you have always wanted to. Or some good news is coming your way.

New ideas are coming into your head. This is a great time of abundance in all areas of your life.

Stop procrastinating on what or when, and just do it. This is the sign you have been looking for. No more holding yourself back – go for it, as Lady Luck is on your side. You can't fail.

Affirmation: *Lady Luck is on my side.*

31 - HAMSTER – *Fun*

I have come to you today to ask, Are you having enough fun?

Has life taken over?

You must bring more fun into your life, as life has been getting you down lately. This is a time where you need to bring the childlike wonder. We can let life get in the way at times. Sit with yourself and remember the fun you had as a child and the wonder of it all. The free nature of the child – this is the energy you should bring into your life.

Do something that you used to do as a child – colour, play ball, roll in the grass, splash in a puddle – and see how it feels and how easy it can be. We get so caught up in it all that we forget to see the fun and enjoyment in the little things. Go have some fun.

Affirmation: *I allow myself to have fun today and every day.*

32. RAT – *Dedication*

I have come to you today to ask, Have you set the right goals for yourself, or have you set any at all?

It is time to get clear on what you want in your life and set the right goals for yourself. When we get clear on what we want, we have some direction to move in.

Be very clear on what you truly want – no holding yourself back. This is where your dreams come true when you set the goals. Set them and start making your move towards them. You don't have to know the how, where, and when you are going to reach it. There is no stopping yourself. Just know that every step you take brings you closer to fulfilling your dreams. Be clear on your goals and believe and trust in yourself and your ability to succeed.

Affirmation: *My desired goals are within my reach now.*

33. PIG – *Opportunities*

I have come to you today to say, There are new opportunities and new doors opening for you. You may be a bit apprehensive about it, but that's OK.

Take a long, hard look at what is being presented to you. You may feel unsure at the start, but don't worry. At first, you might not think that this is the right way forward for you – don't let that hold you back.

This is opening you up to a whole new way of living, better than you could ever have wished for. Get out of your own way and allow yourself to move forward. Walk through the open door and take up the opportunities that present themselves to you. This is a once in a lifetime offer, so don't talk yourself out of taking the chance. Go for it, take that leap of faith.

Affirmation: *I leap forward fearlessly now.*

34. HEN – *Curiosity*

I have come to you today to ask, What have you always been curious about?

All through your life, you have had this curiosity; this is the time for you to put curiosity aside and go find out the information.

You will be surprised at what you will unearth, and that's OK, because you are about to find the truth. Go seek the answers that you so desire; let go of the chapter of your life and leave it where it should be – in the past. This will bring a better understanding into your life, and it will let you free yourself from the past. Remember, this is only about you and nobody else. Let go and move forward with great ease.

Affirmation: *Curiosity is one of the best motives.*

35. PEACOCK – *Confidence*

I have come to you to say, Be like the peacock and allow your confidence to shine. Let go of all your self-doubt and fear and allow yourself to step into your true self.

Allow yourself to shine and let go of the old self-beliefs and programmes that have held you back all your life – they are old beliefs and old patterns that no longer serve you.

Allow your self-confidence to be seen. It's time for you to take your rightful place on this Earth. Yes, you can take centre stage in your life and allow the spotlight to shine on you. When we allow our true selves to emerge, we radiate confidence, and our light shines so bright as we take our rightful place on this Earth. Shine your light with confidence now.

Affirmation: *I radiate confidence and allow my light to shine bright now.*

36. DOLPHIN – *Inner Child*

I have come to you today to ask, What is your inner child showing you? Your inner child has been showing you signs that you have been missing. Stop, look, and see the signs that are telling you there is a pattern that keeps coming up and playing out in your life.

The pattern is linked to your inner child; it is an old pattern that no longer serves you. It's time to go within on a deep level and find the root cause of this.

I know it can be hard doing the inner work. We can get so caught up in the logic mind (ego) and talk ourselves out of doing this work. This pattern has come up to be released once and for all so you can move forward in your life. Stop allowing the ego to win; go within and let it go.

Affirmation: *I leave the past where it should be – in the past.*

37 - SHARK – *Bitten Off*

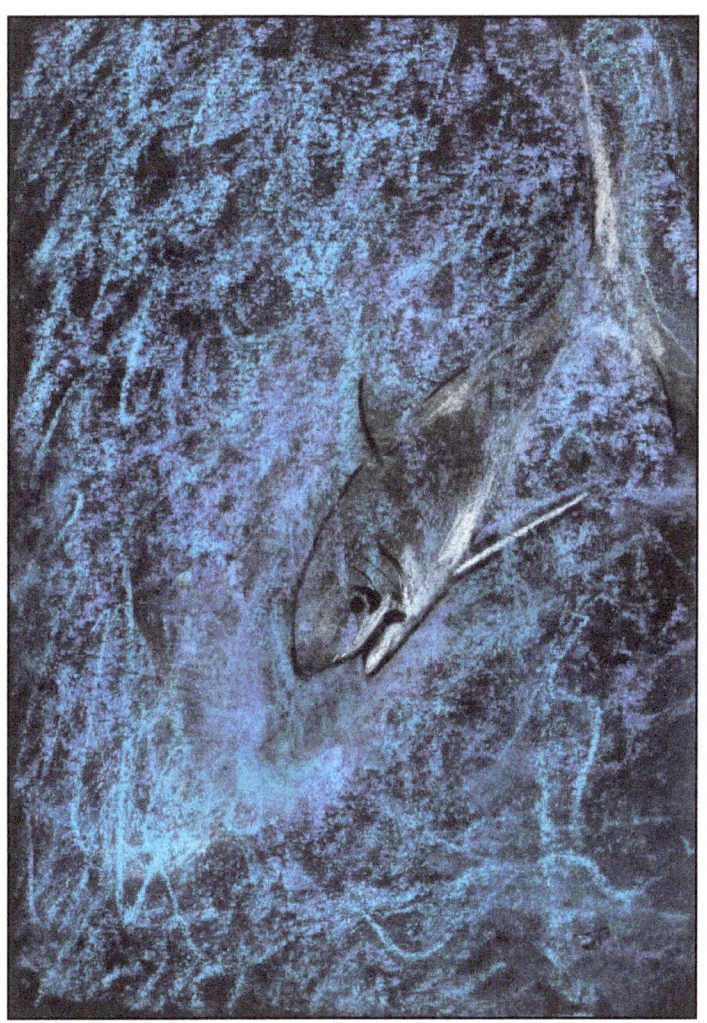

I have come to you today to ask, Have you bitten off more than you can chew?

Have you taken on too much? You are taking on far too much, and you have yourself in a spin. Look at the areas in your life where you can hand over some of the responsibility to someone else; you don't have to do it all yourself.

Hand it over and don't feel guilty about doing this. You cannot keep this up. If you do, you will not be able to take care of yourself, never mind anyone else. This is a sign from spirit to say enough is enough, let it go and let others take their share of the responsibility. This is your time to re-evaluate your life and put yourself first for a change. Ask for the help that you need and allow yourself the easy, carefree life you desire. Let go, hand it over.

Affirmation: *I step back and look after myself now.*

38. WHALE – *Emotions*

I have come to you today to say, I encourage you to embrace your emotions and how they are affecting you and your life. You have buried your emotions for far too long – it is time for them to rise to the surface. I know this can be hard, but to move forward from the past, you must.

Like the whale, dive deep and see where you are holding on to them and allow yourself to go within; allow them to move through the body and, like the water, allow them to wash away. You might find it helpful to write down what you're feeling and just allow what needs to come out, as this will help you release more. The more you release, the better, as it will clear your field to bring new things into your life. So, be brave, go deep and release, and set yourself free from all the emotional baggage you have been carrying far too long.

Affirmation: *I release all my emotional baggage now and set myself free.*

39 - OCTOPUS - *Drive*

I have come to you today to say, I am here to help you to have the drive in your life to go for your goals. I am bringing you new energy; this will help you get up and go for what you truly want in life.

What is holding you back? Is it old beliefs, fear, overthinking? If you just don't know where to start, that's OK. Look at what it is and call me in to help you with this.

I will bring you a new way of seeing how you can take the steps forward, what to do, and fill you full of drive. You can have anything you want; you just need to open yourself up to it and believe and trust in the information that you are getting and take the necessary steps forward. This will bring you all you want.

Affirmation: *I make things happen.*

40. SEAHORSE – *Flow*

I have come to you today to ask, Are you caught up in the how, when, and where, and overthinking every move you have to make? I am here to help you go with the flow.

Allow yourself to be guided in the right direction, like the flow of the current around you, when you see the way to move forward, anchor and ground yourself, and stay focused on your goal.

You have been procrastinating for such a long time and are afraid to move forward. This is your time to fully trust and move forward with flow and ease. If you don't, it will not work. Ease and flow – that is your way forward. This meant to be easy, not hard, but you have been making it hard for far too long. So ground yourself, then make a move forward, and it will all go with ease and flow.

Affirmation: *I move forward with ease and flow.*

41. GOAT – *Guilt*

I have come to you today to say, It's time to release all the guilt that you are holding onto. It is a time of great healing for you. When we hold on to guilt, it goes into the emotions and causes the body to go into dis-ease.

Look at why you are holding on to this guilt and allow yourself to fully forgive yourself. The biggest gift you can give yourself is self-forgiveness. It can be too hard to look at the guilt that we carry, and we can also carry it from a past life or our ancestral lines. Set the intention to clear this once and for all; ask for the help of your guides. Sit with yourself, go deep within, and allow and give yourself permission to release. Set yourself free from guilt; you will feel so much better after you do this, and you can move forward with ease.

Affirmation: *I release all the guilt and I give myself the gift of self-forgiveness.*

42. SNAKE – *Transformation*

I have come to you today to say, This is a time of great transformation for you. You have been waiting for this for a long time. All the inner work you have been doing has brought you to this point in your life. Trust that you are where you should be, you are in the right place at the right time.

We know how hard you have been working to change things and that you may feel tired, and that's OK. You are going through this transformation, and it is taking you to the next level of consciousness. Hang in there, allow it to happen.

If you push, you are pushing it away from you. Just allow it to come to you with ease. You may feel a bit up and down as you go through this but know you will come out the other end. Trust and believe, and all will be OK.

Affirmation: *I get out of my own way and allow myself to go through this transformation with ease.*

43. GORILLA – *Vulnerability*

I have come to you today to ask, Are you feeling a bit vulnerable at the moment?

You may be feeling it on an emotional, physical, or psychic level. This can happen to anyone; the best thing you can do is to see why you are feeling like this. Look at what is causing this and why and make the choice to clear this on all levels. Remember, nobody has any power over you, and you are your own person. You have the power within you to clear this and never let anyone or anything make you feel this way again.

Be like the gorilla: make a stand and take back your power, cut the cords and move forward with confidence. Learn from this and know that you're a very powerful being.

Affirmation: *I fully stand in my divine power with love and light.*

44. CAMEL – *Nurture*

I have come to you today to say, It is time to nurture yourself on all levels. There is a real importance to finding balance in all areas of your life. Take a look at how you can nurture yourself.

Look at the food you eat – is it nurturing your body? Are you eating the right food to keep you in balance? Are you eating junk food that lowers your vibration?

Look at your emotional wellbeing – is that being nurtured? Do you feel good about yourself? Are you able to accept change? Do you have a good balance between work, rest and play? This is very important. Your spiritual practice –how is that? Do you meditate? Do you sit and listen to your guides? This is a very important practice for your wellbeing. Make the change that you need to, you are the only one that can do this.

Affirmation: *I cherish and nurture myself; this brings balance into my life.*

45. GIRAFFE – *Unique*

I have come to you today to ask Have you accepted how unique you are?

Are you hiding your true, unique self from the world?

You have a very unique gift(s) that you are hiding away. It is time to face your fears and let the world see the true you. I know this might be scary at the start. But believe me, once you have done it once, it will be easier the next time.

There is no need to worry about what other people think or say about you – this is none of your business. They are only jealous, and you are only triggering a belief in them. We all have to take a chance in life and see where it will lead us. Don't let fear win, and allow yourself to shine your true uniqueness to the world. No holding yourself back anymore.

Affirmation: *I allow my uniqueness to shine; I take centre stage in my life.*

46. LEOPARD – *Old Issues*

I have come to you today to say, There are old issues popping up in your life again. You haven't fully dealt with them. It is time to sit down and bring these issues to the forefront to be dealt with.

You may be holding on to deep wounds or hurts that you haven't looked at. Look at why and how they are affecting you; sit down with the person or people who have caused you this issue and let them know how this affected you and listen to their side – remember, there are always two sides.

Yes, I know this can be hard, but you must face this head-on for you to heal this and let both of you move forward. It's time to reclaim your power. As this is holding you back, it will keep popping up until you fully deal with it, and there is no time like the present.

Affirmation: *I release all that no longer serves me.*

47. PANDA – *Black and White*

I have come to you today to say Not everything is black and white in life. You need to start looking outside the box. You have been looking at everything with only one view, but there are so many different ways to look at life.

Take a step back and look at how you are viewing your life and the way you handle situations when they come up. Before you make a decision, look around: there are alternative ways.

By stepping back and looking at it from a different viewpoint, the situation will change, and you will see the solution in front of you. It is so easy to get caught up in it all and get into all the drama. We want to see the solution, but it then becomes black and white. This gets us nowhere.

Stop, breathe, step back, and look at it in a different way, and allow the solution to come.

Affirmation: *I think outside the box for solutions.*

48. WORM – *Grounding*

I have come to you today to say, You have become very ungrounded. You need to come back into your body – you seem to be popping out of your body of late.

You need to call your energy back to you from people, places, and situations. When we think of a person, we send out an energetic cord that attaches us to them. We end in their energy, and they end up in ours. By calling your energy back, you take back your energy.

When you call it back, ask for it to come back to a divine filter of pure love and light; you only want your energy back. Once you have done this, ground yourself from the heart chakra down and anchor your energy into the crystal grid of Mother Earth. Also, check in on yourself a few times a day. Make this grounding practice a daily routine.

Affirmation: *I am fully grounded into Mother Earth.*

49. HIPPO – *Questioning Oneself*

I have come to you today to say, Stop questioning yourself. Put the energy you are putting into questioning yourself into believing in yourself instead and see how you can change things for the better.

Trust and believe in you. Press the reset button; this is going to bring a lot of movement and change into all areas of your life.

You have been in the waiting room of your own life for far too long. This energy is affecting all areas of your life. You have come through difficult and challenging situations, and you have learnt lessons from them. You are going through a time of transformation.

Get out of your own way and out of your head. Stop questioning and worrying over how, when, and where it is going to happen; stop pushing and just allow it. What you want, wants you. The only thing you need to do is fully embrace the transformation and allow the change to come in and go with the flow.

Affirmation: *What I want, wants me.*

50. PARROT – *Experience*

I have come to you to ask, What is happening in your life and what you are experiencing are signs from the universe that you need to change things, as the way you are living at this moment in time is not serving you to the fullest.

It may be not eating the right food, not doing your spiritual practice, or not doing enough exercise. Maybe you don't like your job, or you aren't in the right relationship. It is time to look at what you really want in life, and if you don't make the changes, you will keep experiencing the same thing over and over.

We can let life take us over, and sometimes that's OK. It can be hard to change old habits and patterns, but you have the willpower to make changes in your life and start having new life experiences.

Affirmation: *I make the change in my life to bring in new life experiences.*

51. MEERKAT – *Awareness*

I have come to you today to ask, What are you looking at that is taking your awareness away from yourself? You have a tendency to look at what others are doing and compare yourself to them; it's not good for you. Are you getting caught up in it in comparison paralysis? It's not a good energy to hold on to.

Stop. Look at yourself and how far you have come. Stop comparing yourself to others as this only brings you into a negative space which you then find hard to get yourself out of.

It is not your business what other people think of you. You should get on with your own life. Put the energy you have into yourself and see how much you will be able to accomplish and get on with your dreams.

Affirmation: *I focus on myself.*

52. PANDA – *Gentle*

I have come to you today to say, It is time to be gentle with yourself. You are always very hard on yourself, always pushing yourself to the next level in all areas of your life.

For once, give yourself a break, take it easy and chill. Yes, chill. Step back and look at your life from a different point of view and see how it is affecting you.

Change the things that you can and make the time for yourself, even if it's five or ten minutes a day. It will do you the world of good; this will also bring you much-needed balance in all areas of your life. These changes need to be made ASAP, or you will find yourself looking back and asking, 'Where has my life gone?' It will be too late to live the life you want, so stop going and doing. Stop, rest, and chill, and allow yourself to be gentle with yourself.

Affirmation: *I am gentle with myself.*

53. ZEBRA – *Recognition*

I have come to you to say, You are going to get the recognition that you deserve. You have been working so hard to achieve your goals – well done!

You are going to receive a promotion, a new job, or new clients that you so desire. You have been hard at it for a while now. You have sown the seed, and those seeds are about to grow and blossom to their fullest.

Embrace your recognition and give yourself that pat on the back – you deserve it. This is the start of a very good phase in your life. You are about to leave all the old energy behind you and move forward to a positive phase in your life.

Well done for not giving up and for seeing it all through. You are now ready to reap the rewards. Good job!

Affirmation: *I am worthy of recognition and praise.*

54. HEDGEHOG – *Compliance*

I have come to you today to ask, Are you sick of complying with the rules and regulations?

You are finding it hard to stick with all the rules, and that's OK. Rules are made to be broken. The harsh energy of this gets you down at times.

You are asking yourself the questions, 'What good are their rules? Why are they necessary to me and how are they affecting my life?'

Yes, we do have to comply with some rules, but not all of them. You feel at one with yourself when you listen to your inner guidance. When rules don't sit well with you, ask yourself if this rule applies to you. Only you can answer that, so listen, let go, and do what is right for you. We will always make the right choice for you.

Affirmation: *I make the right choice for my highest and greatest good.*

55. POLAR BEAR – *Endurance*

I have come to you today to ask, Are you feeling like giving it all up? You are finding it hard at this time and feeling lost. It's OK to feel like that – we all do, at times.

I am letting you know to hang on in there. I know it hasn't been easy and you feel like just throwing in the towel. DON'T. You have to embrace the storm to break through it. Believe that it is going to happen, even if you can't see how.

Nothing stays the same; I know it might feel like it is, but it doesn't. Look at what you want to change and what action step you should take, and when you feel it's time to move, move forward. You will know when it's the right time: you will be given a sign and the guidance that you need to make the necessary changes. You must put your faith in your guides and allow them to send you the signs, and don't second-guess them. Stay strong, as it's all about to change. You have the strength to get over this.

Affirmation: *This too shall pass.*

56. SEA LION – *Ability*

I have come to you today to say, You have the ability to do anything you want, so what is stopping you? Why are you holding yourself back? You have all the knowledge and wisdom you need within you. Stop looking outside for the answers.

Look how far you have come and how many obstacles you have overcome to get where you are today. Give yourself a pat on the back. Ask yourself if you are happy where you are – or do you want it all and more?

You are the only one that can change and go for what you truly want. Keep telling yourself how far you have come and then get out of your own way. Trust and believe that you can do it, and you will. Allow the life you truly want to unfold before your eyes.

Affirmation: *I have the ability to do anything I want.*

57. ANTELOPE – *Energy*

I have come to you today to say, You need to be very mindful of your energy and keep yourself grounded at all times. You have been popping out of yourself quite easily recently. You need to be 100% in your body.

When you become ungrounded, you go into your head straight away and you let your mind wander; then, all the fear, anxiety, and overwhelm take hold of you, and you are all over the place.

You should check your energy at least twice a day to make sure you don't become ungrounded; as you do this, it will help you get on with your day. Remember to be mindful of your energy. Keep yourself grounded and all will run smoothly and easily. Make decisions from the heart, not the head.

Affirmation: *It is safe for me to be grounded and complete.*

58. CHAMELEON – *Guide*

I have come to you today to say, There is no need to push and try to do everything at one time. You are getting yourself into a state – this does nobody any good at all. It only creates stress and overwhelm.

You must take it a bit easier and allow yourself to be guided. There is no need to hurry or do things all the time – this is a time of rest and rejuvenation.

You have done this all your life, and you find it hard to stop. Ask yourself before you start the day: Do you need to do it all now, or can some of it be put off for another day, or can somebody else do it? When we hand things over to others, we give ourselves permission to look after ourselves, and then this brings us more balance within. Allow yourself to be guided and allow peace and balance into your life.

Affirmation: *I have balance in all areas of my life.*

59. SLOTH – *Patience*

I have come to you today to say, Patience is not your forte. You find it hard to be patient; you want it now, but there are times in our life when we can't have it now. When that happens, we should sit back and let things flow naturally, and this is one of those times.

You have been working so hard. You have planted the seeds, and now is the time to water them. This is your time to look at what you have accomplished and enjoy all the good things in life. Allow the seeds to grow.

So, take this time to practice self-care, whatever that is for you, and be patient. The way the seeds grow may not be the way you want them to, but that's OK – the universe has other plans. Be open to all possibilities; you might think that the way forward doesn't look like the right move, but trust as you will reap the rewards. Have faith, trust, and be patient.

Affirmation: *My patience is growing every day.*

60. DUCK – *Comfort*

I have come to you today to ask, Are you getting too comfortable and allowing life to pass you by, wondering what is next? This is not serving your highest good.

There is a drive in you that you are not meeting. This drive will take you to the next level if you unleash it and get out of your comfort zone. Ask yourself what you want, where you want to go, and tap into your drive. It will give you the passion that you are missing and bring in a whole new way of being. You are the only one that can do this, so stop looking at others to help you. That drive, that passion is within you: unleash it and set yourself free.

Affirmation: *I unleash my drive and passion and set myself free.*

61. DONKEY – *Challenges*

I have come to you today to say, You have been presented with a challenge in your life. Look at the challenge presented to you: Is this a pattern or is it a new one? If it's a pattern, it's time to release it once and for all. Look at the pattern and ask yourself how long this has been presenting itself. Is it years, past lives, ancestral, or this lifetime? We can take on other people's challenges without knowing we are doing it.

See what emotions are attached to it, what triggers it, and why it triggers. Sit and journal on how it is making you feel, or why it is making you feel this way. Do the inner work and start to see this in a different light and then you will see this challenge change. You will then be able to clear it out of your life once and for all. We are all faced with challenges; it's how we handle them that is important. Holding onto them is no good because they become a pattern and they are hard to release, so do yourself a favour: let it go, and set yourself free.

Affirmation: *I let go of all challenges in my life and set myself free.*

62. CRAB – *Holding On*

I have come to you today to ask, What are you holding on to that is not serving you? You have the tendency to hold onto old emotions as if your life depended on it. This is not serving you well; it is causing you dis-ese in your body and, in some way, is causing you to be ill.

This is your time to let go and surrender all these old emotions you have been holding onto most of your life. You may not know how to do this, and that's OK. On some level, the emotions have become a security blanket, and fear will hold this in place.

Call on your angels, guides, spirit, loved ones, or me – the crab – to help show you how to surrender these emotions to the divine. We will give you guidance on how to do this with practices like meditation, yoga, journaling, and contemplation. You will receive the guidance you need to help you release, surrender, and set yourself free to move forward along your path.

Affirmation: *I give myself permission to release all that no longer serves me, and I set myself free.*

63. WASP – *Held Back*

I have come to you today to ask, Are you tired of feeling held back by people, situations, or circumstances? If so, this is your time to let it all go and take control of your own life.

Stop allowing others to affect your life and start living the life you want. Start by making a list of what and who is holding you back, and then take your power back from them.

Look at the changes you want to bring in and start making plans on how and when you are going to make these changes. Start by making small changes as they lead to the big ones; be gentle with yourself as you do this, as even the smallest of changes can have a huge impact on our lives.

You are the one holding yourself back by allowing others to do this to you. The most important thing is that you are aware of this and can make the change you want and move forward with ease.

Affirmation: *I am in charge of how I feel, so I choose happiness.*

64. FLY – *Listening*

I have come to you today to ask, What are or aren't you listening to? You are ignoring guidance and signs on a daily basis. Either you can't see them, or you are, on some level, blocking the information coming to you. This may be caused by fear. There is no need to fear this information – it is for your highest good. We come with these signs to help you move forward. Know that we are with you, and we are assuring you. You are on the right path.

Open yourself up, let go of the fear, and allow us into your life, as we can help you move forward. Know that we are guiding you with ease in the right direction. We will never lead you along the wrong path, because we only have your best interests at heart.

Open your eyes and see the wonder of the world around you and allow yourself to see the signs we are sending you. As you do this, the magic will unfold within you. Let go of fear and listen.

Affirmation: *I open myself to seeing the signs of the universe.*

65. BUTTERFLY – *Transcend*

I have come to you today to say, It's your time to go beyond your limits. I am bringing you to new heights.

I am opening you up to a new way of being; the only thing you should do is trust in the process to happen. The way you see, feel, and experience life is about to change. There is a whole new energy opening up to you, and this energy will help you evolve to the next level of consciousness.

Yes, it's going to be a bumpy ride, but don't worry. You are ready for this. You can't stay where you are, and this needs to happen for you to go to the next level.

Patterns, paradigms, and old beliefs will come out to be surrendered and released. You have to let go; the new energy that is coming in will help you transcend to the next level of consciousness. The old way of doing things will no longer serve you. Let go of the old, embrace the new, trust and believe the universe has your back as you transcend to the next level.

Affirmation: *The universe has my back, now and always.*

66. PENGUIN – *Teamwork*

I have come to you today to say, You have a lot of new ideas coming in; some of them are for you to work with others. Sit with these new ideas and ask your guide who is the person you are to do this work with, and trust.

Don't rush into anything; give yourself time to think it fully through and make sure this is the right person. Deep down, you will know the answer. You will be guided to this person. There is also an expansion of your business on some level with a partnership coming into you; this will bring the business to the next level.

Make sure you get legal advice and make sure you read the small print before signing. This new partnership is going to bring a new energy into your life, and it will allow you to bring your dreams forward. You will blossom with this new venture together.

Affirmation: *Together, we achieve more.*

67. OSTRICH – *Burying*

I have come to you today to ask, What are you burying and afraid to look at? Take your head out of the sand and really look at what is going on.

You have a tendency to not look at things head-on; you ignore them, hoping they will go away, but this is going nowhere. The more you ignore this, the worse it will get, and it will be harder to deal with.

Open your eyes and see what is really going on and face it head-on. It is the only way. You have been burying your head most of your life and not dealing with things, and yes, some have just gone away, but not this time. It is here to stay until you deal with it, once and for all.

Yes, I know fear can stop you, but this time you must face it. Allow yourself to feel the fear and face it anyway. You will become a much stronger person when you do this, so take your head out of the sand, stand on your own two feet and face it head-on, and trust in the process.

Affirmation: *I face my fears head-on with love.*

68. CROCODILE – *Hard Exterior*

I have come to you today to say, You have a hard exterior that you show the world. You find it hard to trust people, and it takes you a long time to let anyone in – or do you ever let them fully in at all? This hard exterior no longer serve you.

It is time to drop the wall of defence and allow your true self to shine. You are a very loving person behind that hard exterior. Allow the world and yourself to see this beautiful, caring person that you are.

It's time to heal. Allow your heart to expand and love yourself unconditionally as this is your way forward. When we love ourselves, we drop the hard exterior we have built up over time, and this is your time to knock them down. Remember to be gentle as you go through this, and you are unconditionally loved.

Affirmation: *I love and accept myself exactly as I am.*

69. EMU – *Excellence*

I have come to you today to say, It is time to devote your time to your spiritual excellence. You are a teacher who has all the wisdom and knowledge within you, but you just can't see it yet. You are trying to ignore it out of fear. You are being guided to sit and call me in to guide you through this process of spiritual excellence. The only way to get through this is to follow the guidance and allow your true path to open up in front of you.

You will be given a daily practice to do and over time you will perfect this. Stop doubting and allow. The only person that can stop you going through this is yourself. Don't let fear hold you back; this is your life purpose, and you know that deep down this is perfect for you. This is what you have been asking for and the direction will unfold when you are ready. Be the spiritual teacher you have come here to be and allow the true you to emerge.

Affirmation: *I allow my true self to emerge now.*

70. KANGAROO – *New Path*

I have come to you today to say, You have been asking for a sign for a while; know that this is your sign. The answer is yes. It is time to move forward. You have been complaining for a while and asking for something new to come in for you, like a new course, new job, or new relationship.

There is a clear path opening up for you at this time, but you must take the necessary steps forward. There is no point in hanging on any longer – there are no obstacles in your way, the path is clear. You have done the inner work that allows you to have a clear path ahead. Congratulations on going into the deepest parts of yourself and giving yourself that time to heal all that needed to heal to get you where you are today. Congratulations for listening to your inner self and guides.

Affirmation: *My path ahead is clear.*

71. KOALA BEAR – *Take it Easy*

I have come to you today to say, It's time for you to sit back and relax; you have come so far, and you have been doing so much. This is your time to reap the rewards.

Your hard work has paid off, and you are going to enjoy the fruits of your labour. You have overcome all the fear and doubt, and you have succeeded. Now is the time to kick off your shoes and take it easy.

Enjoy some quiet time with family and friends or read a book that you have been putting off for a while. While you take this time out of your busy life and rest, a new set of ideas will come in.

The new ideas could not come while you were too busy looking after all the other things; now, while you rest, they will just drop in with ease. Rest and relaxation is the order of the next few days for you.

Affirmation: *I allow myself to rest and relax.*

72. PORCUPINE – *Chaos*

I have come to you today to ask, Has life been chaotic for you for a while now? You have been letting everything get to you, and you seem to be running around after yourself yet can't seem to get anywhere.

The first thing you need to do is to ground and bring yourself back to centre. Call all your energy back to you – you are scattered all over the place, attached to people, places, and things. Once you call all your energy back and ground, you will feel a lot better.

You must do this on a daily basis and check in with yourself twice a day and make sure you are grounded and in your body. Then you can make the changes that you want so you don't have to be chasing your tail all the time. Once you have done this, you will be able to enjoy your life and let go of the chaos around you.

Affirmation: *I allow myself to ground and be at one with myself.*

73. COYOTE – *Guide*

I have come to you today to say, You have a new guide waiting to connect with you; they have been waiting in the wings for a while now. They have been sending you signs for a while now. You are missing them, and they have a lot of guidance to give you.

To open yourself up to the guide, sit with yourself and ask for them to make their presence known. Feel, see, or sense them around you; ask them their name and what they have come to help you with. Trust in the information you are receiving. (Always trust that the first thing that comes into your head is the guidance or the answer you have been asking about. When we start second-guessing the information, that's when the ego has kicked in – we get lost in ourselves and let doubt and fear creep in.) Do this on a regular basis and build up the trust within you. Follow the guidance that you are receiving and just allow it to unfold.

Affirmation: *I trust and believe in the guidance I receive.*

74. RACOON – *Problem Solved*

I have come to you today to say, You have been asking for a problem to be solved for some time now. You just can't seem to get past this; have our learnt your lesson yet? Ask yourself the question, 'What is the lesson to be learned around this?' Be honest with yourself. If you can't be honest with yourself, then who can you be honest with? When you see the lesson and then ask for help, you will see the solution to this problem.

You should trust the information that you receive around this and take the action that is necessary for you to overcome this.

This will not solve itself unless you see the lesson; the problem will keep rearing its head over and over until you see the lesson and learn from it. The only one that can do this is you; you have the courage within you to go there.

Affirmation: *I turn my lessons into blessings.*

75. CHEETAH – *Speed*

I have come to you today to ask, Why is everything in your life done with speed? Why are you not allowing yourself to go with the flow?

You are always in a hurry to get things done, and there is always a lot of endurance with all that you do. You are being guided to stop and look at how you are conducting yourself in all that you do, and slow down. When you are doing and not flowing, you are missing all the signs and messages that are being sent to you.

This is the way you have gone through most of your life to get by, but no more, as this is stopping you from being who you truly are. Ask yourself what or who are you running from.

When you get the answer, allow yourself to go deep within and release all that is holding you and holding on to this pattern. Let go and surrender – it will do you the power of good. The real you will emerge from this; you can slow down, live a life with less stress, and allow your life to flow with ease.

Affirmation: *I allow myself to be my truest divine self.*

76. JAGUAR – *Inner Power*

I have come to you today to help you reclaim your inner power by reawakening your inner core energy. It is time to let go of all the old emotions that you are holding onto in your mind, body, and soul. It's time to reclaim your true self.

You must sit and call me, along with your other guides, and allow yourself to bring up the past that is holding you back. Allow yourself to feel it coming up and feel the emotion on all levels, then let go and surrender. This is not an easy task, but if you want your true self to awaken, then this is a must.

You have great strength and courage within you; allow all that needs to come to the surface and release. Let go. We would not ask you to do this if we didn't think you had it within you to overcome this. Allow the true divine self to emerge and stand in your true power.

Affirmation: *I reclaim my personal power now.*

77. LYNX – *Moon Energy*

I have come to you today to say, It is time for you to fully embrace your moon energy. You are very sensitive to the moon's energy, and it affects you in all areas of your life.

You should start working with the moon cycles and allow yourself to use the moon to manifest your dream and desires. During the full moon and new moon, take note of how you are feeling – you will start to see a pattern develop of how the different moon phases affect you.

You have the ability to tap into the moon's energy and see how it is going to work for you; it's like the moon is talking to you. You will have your own unique way of working with the moon, and you will know how to use it to manifest, which will bring you great success. You have used the moon before in a past life; you are reawakening this within you, and you will remember how and when to use the moon magic. This will become second nature to you; get out of your own way and allow the moon magic to unfold and bring you the success you desire.

Affirmation: *I allow myself to unlock the moon magic within.*

78. OTTER – *Joy*

I have come to you today to say, There is a need to bring more joy into your life; you have been letting life get you down. We all do that from time to time, but you just can't seem to get out of this.

First off, start seeing the joy in the little things in life. Be grateful for all that you have and look at what brings you joy in your life. When we see and feel the joy within ourselves, we start attracting more into our lives.

You have let life get you down; this is your time to get up and bring in the joy, fun, and laughter. It's time to enjoy life again. When we have joy, our heart expands, so allow yourself to have and see it within you, and you will start attracting more of it into your life. Remember – like attracts like.

Affirmation: *I see and feel the joy in my life.*

79. MOOSE – *Pride*

I have come to you today to ask, Has your pride been knocked? Do you feel let down by yourself or others? We can all feel this way at times, when things don't work out the way we think they should have.

It is time to put this behind you and start afresh by forgiving yourself or others. There is no point in dwelling on this, as it is only holding you back. There is so much more out there for you.

Stop blocking yourself and letting your pride get in the way. This is a time for you to get up, get on with it, and get out of your own way. Leave the past mistakes behind where they should be – left in the past where they belong, not holding you back.

We all have our pride, and it does get knocked every so often. We must get up, dust it off, and get on with our lives, and this is one of those times for you.

Affirmation: *I take pride in myself and all that I do.*

80. ELK – *Rut*

I have come to you today to ask, Are you often getting yourself stuck in a rut and can't seem to get out of your own way, allowing your life to pass you by? This can happen to anyone.

The first thing you should do is see what you want to do. What is your next move? Are you happy with all you have? Do you want more on all levels?

Ask your guides to help with this. Ask for a sign on what direction you need to move in and what action you must take and trust the information that you are receiving.

The best thing that you can do is start doing a daily practice like meditation, yoga, walking, or sitting with your guides. You will receive the information that you need. It's easy to fall back into the rut, but it's up to you to make the changes, keep moving forward, and allow yourself to receive the guidance that you need to keep yourself from falling back into the rut.

Affirmation: *I take the necessary steps forward.*

81. HOG – *New Life*

I have come to you today to say, This is a time of great change for you. You are on the cusp of birthing something new; it may be a new relationship, new job, new home, or even starting your own business.

You have so much to offer the world. Stop pushing – sit back and let it come to you. When we push, we push it away, but when we sit back, it flows to us.

You are being given a new lease on life, and this is going to bring all the new beginnings into your life. Stop, look around, see what you truly want, then make a wish; allow it to flow to you. This is the birth of a much-wanted child, a miracle child. This is a time of great excitement for you, so enjoy every moment.

Affirmation: *I allow myself to birth the new into my life.*

82. LIZARD – *Cycles*

I have come to you today to say, We go through many cycles in our lives, and you are coming to the end of one. It's time to move forward into a new cycle – you could be going back to study, it could be a change in career, or a spiritual awakening. When we go through these cycles every seven years, our direction in life changes.

Take a look at what worked for you and what didn't work and let go of what is holding you back. This is why you have been feeling a bit out of sorts lately.

You are going through these changes, and there is no holding on to the past. You must release this old energy to move forward to the new exciting ventures waiting for you. Go ahead toward the next step into the new cycles of your life, as this will bring you more happiness and joy. No more holding yourself back.

Affirmation: *I embrace the changes upon me.*

83. SCORPION – *Self-Protection*

I have come to you today to say, You are being guided to protect your energy, as you are picking up other people's energy, but you are not clearing their energy out of your body. You are an empath; you can sense, feel, and take on other people's energy, but most of the time, you don't even know you are doing this.

This is affecting you on all levels. You are feeling down, tired, and drained. Your mood can get low, and you don't know what is causing it. It's because you are so open to other people's feelings and emotions and you can take them on, so you must ground, clear your energy, and protect yourself on a daily basis.

By doing this, you will feel so much better in yourself as you will only be dealing with your own emotion and energy. It's so important that you do this daily practice of clearing, grounding, and protecting as it will keep you from picking up unwanted energy. Also, check in with yourself after being in a crowd as this will really affect you.

Affirmation: *I am the only master of my energy.*

84. GOLDFISH – *Prosperity*

I have come to you today to say, There is good luck and good fortune on its way to you. You can turn your hand to anything at the moment, and it will turn to gold; this is a very prosperous time in your life.

You can turn your life around and make your dreams come true – go for the gold! You have the energy of success around you at the moment, and it's about to create you a successful future.

Start by dreaming big and then go for it – you can't lose. You will be at the top of your game, and your biggest dreams and desires are about to come true. You have been waiting and working towards this for some time now. You never gave up, even when the self-doubt crept in, and you still hung in there. Now it's time to reap your rewards, and you are about to reach the finish line. Congratulations for all your hard work!

Affirmation: *I prosper in all areas of my life.*

85. WOMBAT – *Foundation*

I have come to you today to say, This is your time to build your foundation. If we don't have a strong foundation, we can't build on it, or it won't hold what we want it to hold, and it will all come tumbling down.

It might feel like you are getting nowhere, and you may even feel you are stuck and can't seem to move forward. All is not what it seems; you are being asked to build your foundations and build them strong. When we have a strong foundation, nothing can knock us down.

I know you can't see the direction you are going in, but we – your guides – are working away in the background on what you truly want in life. Before we can bring this to you, you must do the work on your foundation in life.

Make it strong and steady; go into your core by way of meditation, yoga, or whatever you are guided to. If you don't know how to do this, just ask your guides, trust the information, and take action.

Affirmation: *I am the architect of my life; I build my foundation.*

86. CHIPMUNK – *Restless*

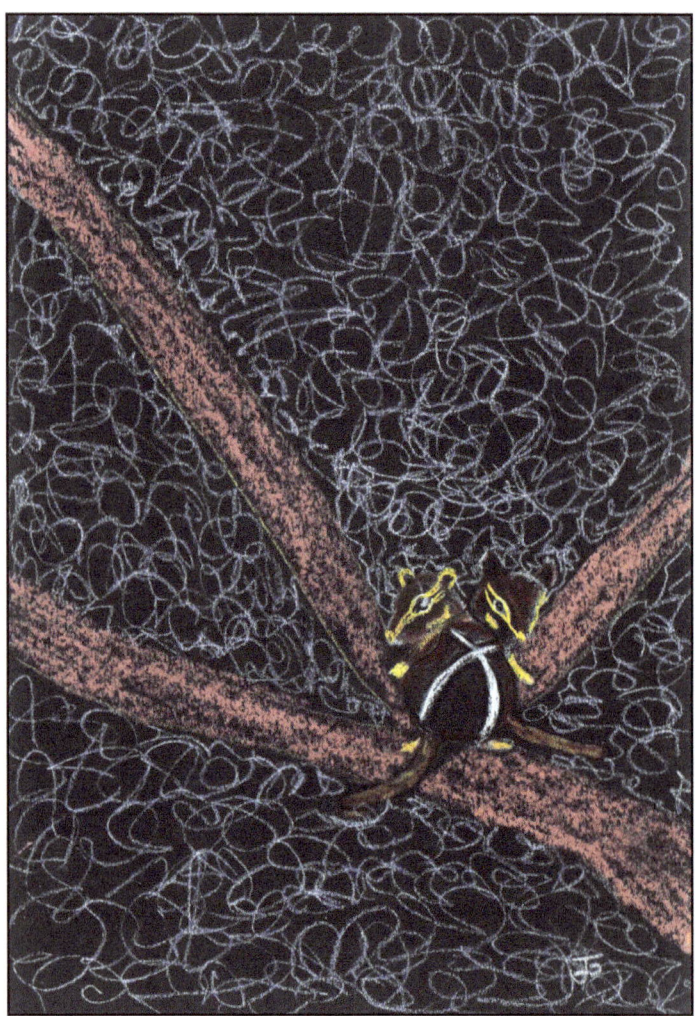

I have come to you today to ask, Are you feeling restless at the moment? Can't seem to keep focused on anything? Jumping from one thing to another? Can't seem to get what you are looking for?

You have been looking in the wrong place all this time; what you are looking for is within you. You just can't see it. Go within and find your true magic. Allow yourself to let go of all the old emotional baggage, patterns, and conditioning. Allow it all out and set yourself free.

Your wisdom has been within you all the time you were looking outside for the answer, and this was causing you to become more restless. I know this is not going to be easy, unlocking your wisdom and magic. It's not an easy road that you must go down, to expand to your next level of consciousness and allow your true divine self to emerge.

Affirmation: *I have the strength to go within to unleash my true divine self.*

87. POSSUM – *Lay Low*

I have come to you today to say, This is a time in your life when you need to just lay low. You have said or done something you regret, and you can't take it back. We all do things in life that we regret; we can let our heads rule our hearts.

You never meant to hurt this person. They may be feeling quite hurt, yet they know what you said/did was the right thing – but the way you did it wasn't. Give them time to get over this, and they will come around.

Let them come to their own conclusion by themselves; they will need time. Let go of this situation and give it time to heal; it will heal, but it will take time. Let go of the need to control.

Affirmation: *I allow healing to happen in this situation.*

88. HYENA – *Strong Willed*

I have come to you today to say, Sometimes being strong-willed does not do you any good; you can get so stuck in your ways that you can't see what is really happening. You have a tendency to hang onto things, and this does not serve you well.

It is time to be more open and see other people's perspectives on things. Allow yourself to look at all sides before making your mind up; you don't seem to listen to others before you make your decision.

You have a very open heart; allow people to see that side of you, and you will get on much better. Allow that strong will to be put aside as this doesn't serve you anymore – it did once, but not now.

Affirmation: *I allow my gentler side to be seen.*

89. CHIMPANZEE – *Committed*

I have come to you today to ask, Are you fully committed to your spiritual awakening? Do you really want this?

Or are you just going through the motions and wondering why you are getting nowhere? The question you need to ask yourself is, Do you really want this?

If the answer is yes, then you must sit with yourself and do the inner work. Get yourself a daily practice – if you don't know what that is, ask your guides to help, or maybe get a mentor that can help you.

Be accountable for your daily actions. The more you sit with yourself, the more you release, the more you evolve – you already know this, you just got complacent. Know that this is your time to get back to doing what you do best. Doing self-care, creating the best version of yourself, and being committed is the way you will achieve this – no holding yourself back.

Affirmation: *I am fully committed to being the best version of myself.*

90: JELLYFISH – *Faith*

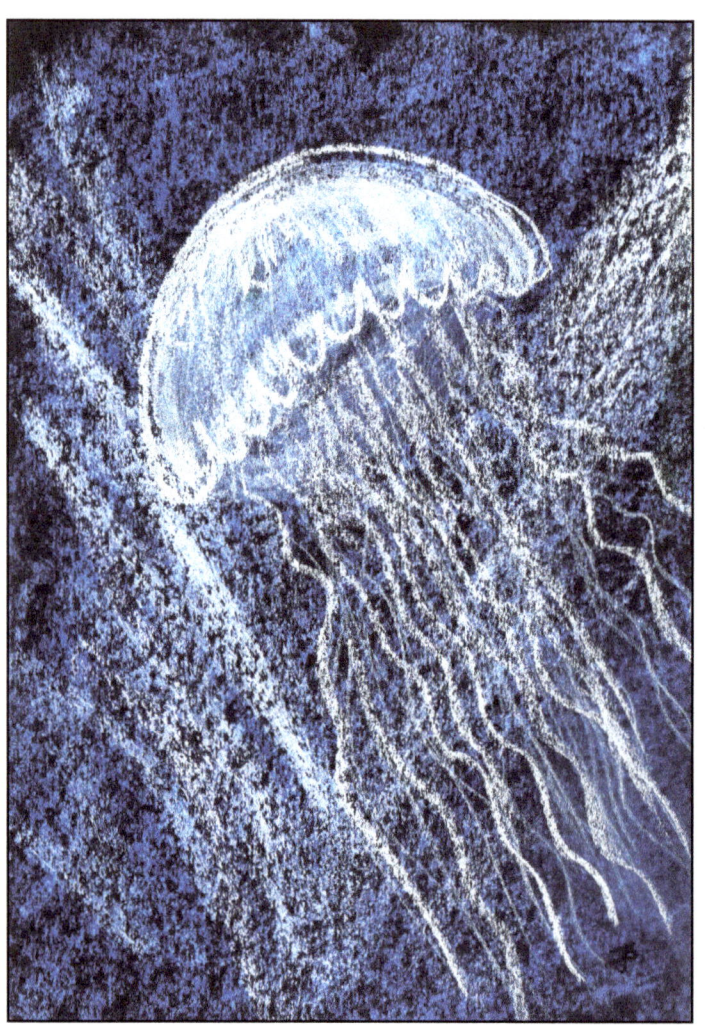

I have come to you today to say, It is time for you to have faith in all that is occurring at this time. You are at the right place, and at the right time. I know you want more, and you will get more, but not yet.

We are working away in the background. We ask you to trust, believe, and have faith as we lead you along the right path.

There will be two paths opening up for you, and the choice is yours and yours alone. We can guide you only if you ask, but the final decision will be yours. Both paths will lead you to the same results, but one will be easier than the other, so choose wisely.

No matter what path you choose, we will walk alongside you, helping and guiding you. Hold on to the faith and trust, and believe in yourself. You will make the right decision – no decision is wrong. Have faith in us and yourself.

Affirmation: *I have faith in myself and the universe.*

91. BAT – *Shadow Side*

I have come to you today to say, It is time to face your shadow side and release all that no longer serves you. We all have a shadow side to us; this is the side of us that we don't want anyone to see. There can be good things we don't like about ourselves.

Look at the shadow side of yourself that you have been hiding from yourself and others. See why you are doing this, go deep within, and be at one with yourself. We need to get in touch with the different sides of ourselves and make peace within them. It's not easy doing the shadow work; it can bring up lost memories that you may have buried, and they can have deep wounds associated with them.

Be gentle with yourself as you release the shadow within you. This can bring on the dark night of the soul but remember that you are going to get through this, and there is light at the end of the tunnel as you embrace your shadow.

Affirmation: *I embrace my shadow and release all that no longer serves me now.*

92. HARE – *Femininity*

I have come to you today to say, I have come to help you embrace your divine feminine side; you have been running on the male side for far too long now. It's time to embrace the divine feminine.

Allow your gentle side to come out; this will help you fully express who you truly are. It may be as simple as putting on some makeup daily, dressing in a feminine way, doing your nails, and allowing it to unfold.

You will see the gentler side of yourself emerging as you do this. You can be so hard on yourself at times, yet you can be very gentle with others. You must bring this gentleness to yourself as well. Show yourself some compassion and allow the soft side of you to emerge.

Embrace both sides of yourself; this is who you truly are. Allow yourself to love yourself unconditionally.

Affirmation: *I unleash my true, divine, feminine self.*

93. FROG – *Hop to it*

I have come to you today to say, Yes, I said hop to it! What is holding you back? This is what you have been waiting on for such a long time now, yet now you are hesitant to move forward.

Now that you have what you want, you're afraid to embrace this. This opportunity will not be around for too much longer; in fact, it may never come around again, so don't let fear hold you back.

Ask yourself the question, *Is this what you truly want*? You are the only one who can answer this question. Sit down and write out the pros and cons and make your decision on this, but don't take too long as it may not be there when you go back to it.

Yes, it can be hard to make the right choice, but once you make the decision, there is no going back and your decision will be final, so let go of the fear.

Affirmation: *I make my decision and move forward with ease.*

94. MOLE – *Fresh Air*

I have come to you today to say, It is time that you get out and get some fresh air and connect with nature. Fresh air is important to you, as it will bring you a sense of renewal.

It will also keep you grounded, and you will receive messages from the elements when you are out there. When out in the fresh air, take a deep breath and allow the oxygen to energise your body.

You will feel much better in yourself by spending time outside; it will uplift your mood. Connect with the elementals as they have important messages for you.

They will also help you recharge your mind, body, and spirit, help you release all the weary energy that you are holding onto, and bring you back into your true divine self.

Affirmation: *I let go of all that no longer serves me now.*

95. ANT – *Willpower*

I have come to you today to say, You have very strong willpower; this can help you in all areas of your life.

You can use this to your advantage -- when you set your mind to something, you must go for it, and your willpower kicks in naturally.

Are you using it in all areas of your life? You can use it in your business and your spiritual growth. Look at what you want and make a plan; when you set your plan, anchor it and allow your willpower to come into play. You will see the difference in your drive when you do this.

You must get the balance right, because you can overdo it, and you can easily burn yourself out. When that happens, you will be no good to anyone and you will find it hard to get back on track. Be careful and make sure you get the balance right. When the balance is right, you will be surprised how easily you can achieve your goals and how life can just flow.

Affirmation: *I have limitless drive and willpower.*

96. BEETLE – *Diet*

I have come to you today to say, You have become very sensitive to certain foods, so now you must watch what foods you are eating and how they are affecting you.

Be careful – you may be sensitive to a lot of processed foods. They are affecting your energy level, sleeping patterns, your mood and your digestive system. It might just be that your vibration has gotten higher, and you have become sensitive to a lot of foods.

The best thing you can do is keep a diary of what foods you are eating, how they are affecting you, and cutting on the ones that are not good for you anymore. It's going to be trial and error for a while until you know what your body can handle.

Affirmation: *Healthy eating is a way of life; it comes easily to me.*

97. TORTOISE – *Easy Does It*

I have come to you today to say, This is your time to take it easy; you have been rushing around for far too long now. This running around has become a bit of a habit, but there is no need to do it all yourself.

Lighten your load and give some of the responsibility to others. You must rest up now as your life is about to change for the better. You cannot bring in this change if you are running around after everyone and everything.

You have been looking to bring in these changes for a while, but you couldn't because you have been too busy. Now is the time to hand it all over and rest; take it easy for once and allow the changes that need to take place.

Yes, it might be hard to rest, but it will be worth every bit of it, and you will be able to bring in that much-needed balance in all areas of your life.

Affirmation: *I allow myself to rest and bring in the changes I want.*

98. SNAIL – *Stress*

I have come to you today to say, Oh, you have put yourself under so much stress. You are overthinking everything you do, and you can't seem to get anything right at this moment. You have let life get on top of you. That's OK. We can all do that at times; you must look at what the cause is or what triggers you.

When we look at why and what is affecting us and causing stress, we can do something about it, and that is half the battle. You are the only one that can change how you are feeling and how it is affecting you.

Do the inner work, forgive, and let it all go. Get out of your head and drop into your heart; keep yourself grounded at all times, as this will help you stay out of your head. This has become a pattern in your life; when you are aware that you are overthinking, ask yourself if this serves you. Allow yourself to ground, drop into the heart, and change the thought. It will take you a while to bring this new pattern in, but when it becomes second nature to you, your life will flow with ease and grace.

Affirmation: *I am willing to change.*

99. SWAN – *Soulmate*

I have come to you today to say, You have or are about to meet your soulmate; this can be on a romantic level or friendship. You will know straight away when this person comes into your life.

This is a connection that is like no other you have had before. This person gets you on all levels; you will have mutual respect for each other, and it's like you have known this person all your life.

They will be right by your side as you go through life's up and downs, and vice versa. This connection will be on a very deep level, and you will blossom together – it's like the missing piece of the puzzle.

This connection will come into your life just at the right time, as there are a lot of changes going on for you at this time. It's like you have your very own safety blanket with this person, and they will feel the same about you.

Affirmation: *I attract my soulmate into my life now.*

100. WOODPECKER – *Family Life*

I have come to you today to say, There is a new addition or change coming to your family – a new baby, a puppy, or even somebody moving out, or a child going to college or buying their first home.

There is a lot of excitement around this, and it's bringing a lot of change within your family. You may be feeling a bit stressed about all this change, and that's OK. Call on me, the woodpecker, and I will help you through this.

Change within the family can be hard to experience at times; we want our family to do so well but not at the expense of moving away from us. It is something you are just going to have to get used to as the changes are happening; it will also bring a lot of love into your family.

Embrace the changes and be gentle with yourself and everyone else as you go through this time.

Affirmation: *I embrace the changes that are coming to my family with love.*

101. SALMON – *Movement*

I have come to you today to say, This is a great time of movement for you; you may have been feeling stuck or even a bit lost, but not for much longer.

You are opening up to a lot of changes coming your way on all levels; it's like your stars have aligned at the right time. I know you have been waiting for this for some time now. You were doubting yourself and your ability.

There is no need for that doubt anymore. I am showing you the way forward now, so leave the fear, self-doubt, and all the bullshit you have been telling yourself behind you and get ready for the energy of movement.

New ideas, opening doors, or a partnership will be presented to you. No holding yourself back, as this is what you have been asking for. Call on me to show you your first step towards your dream and desires – it is all waiting for you.

Affirmation: *I allow myself to move forward with ease and grace.*

102. LIONESS – *Carefree*

I have come to you today to ask, You are holding on too far too much, and you are letting yourself get stressed and anxious. You may feel like you can't seem to keep yourself up; when something happens, it just knocks you down again and again.

You can't seem to let go, and when you do, you are not letting it all go, and this is what is knocking you down all the time. The key to this is to stop yourself before your feelings take you over; when this happens, you go into overwhelm and can't realign yourself. Call on the lioness when you feel the emotions rising. Breathe, feel my presence, and allow the emotions to come up, but this time as they come up, give yourself permission to let them go. You have the strength of the lioness within you to release all you need.

So, breathe through it, allow the emotions to surface, feel them, and let them go. As you do this every time something happens, life becomes carefree and easy as you are no longer holding on.

Affirmation: *I am relaxed and carefree.*

103. BEAGLE – *God*

I have come to you today to say, 'Dog' backwards spells 'God', man's best friend. I am loyal, and I will protect you as you go along your spiritual journey. God is connected with you all the time and will help you find your own path in life.

You must connect with me on a daily basis, as I have so much insight to give you as you go along your path. You may be feeling a bit disillusioned at the moment about what or where is your direction in life. I am sending you more guides to teach you how to fully connect and unleash your inner wisdom; gifts that have been forgotten will be remembered. As you reawaken and remember, your life's path/ journey will become clearer.

Trust and believe that you have a mission in life, and you are about to embark on this mission. The key to your success is listening, believing and trusting in the information you receive and following the guide without question, as I will never lead you astray.

Affirmation: *I am God and God is always with me.*

104. CAT – *Standing in Your Power*

I have come to you today to say, It's time to fully stand in your own power. Stop letting others walk all over you; you need to stand up for what you believe in and what you want out of life. Are you going to be in other people's shadows all your life?

I, the cat, will always get what I want, and I will help you get what you want.

You need to step into your power and believe that you can do this. Stop listening to negative thoughts and beliefs that others have projected onto you.

Cats are very resourceful, so connect with me, and I will show you the way to be resourceful. It's time to look at how others are holding you back, how much control they have over you, and if this relationship is serving you and your dreams. Only you can answer that – be honest with your answer. Take your power back and start living your life and fulfilling your dreams – not others'.

Affirmation: *I stand in my own power with love.*

105. STALLION – *Fenced In*

I have come to you today to say, It is time to let yourself out of the coral you have yourself in. You have been fenced in for far too long now, and it's time to set yourself free.

You keep stopping yourself – you get so far, but then you go back in and lock the door behind you. You have done this a few times now, and the horse is saying, 'Enough is enough!' You need to be free and acknowledge this to help you move forward.

The next time you break free, there is no turning back. This is the last time; you must move forward. The only thing holding you back is yourself, nobody else. You need to do this for yourself – set yourself free, nobody can do this for you.

There is no time like the present; break free, do what your heart desires, have faith, trust and believe in yourself, and move forward. No looking back.

Affirmation: *I set myself free.*

106. FIELD MOUSE – *Low Self-Esteem*

I have come to you today to say, You are quiet, a shy person who stands behind others. You never speak up for yourself; you are very timid and allow others to walk all over you.

You need to stand up for yourself, need to be heard and seen. You always like not to be seen and never like being in the spotlight.

You feel nobody listens to you; the mouse is saying, 'No more.' It is your time to shine your light; it's buried very deep within, and it's very dim. You must feed your light and let it shine.

The way to do this is to speak up for yourself. Let your opinion be heard and step out of the shadow of others; you have a lot to say, and you need to be heard. You just need to believe in yourself: you can do this; the world is waiting for your light to shine and shine bright.

Affirmation: *I allow my light to shine and shine bright.*

107. WHITE RABBIT – *Stop Hiding!*

I have come to you today to say, The rabbit has come to say, 'Stop hiding!' Come out of your burrow and see what the world has to offer you. You seem to be lurking in the dark; you must step out into the light as fear is stopping you. You are in a bit of a low place in life, and you can only see the dark. You have tunnel vision; you must look around as there is so much more of the world to see.

You must step out, let yourself shine in all areas of your life. You seem to do a lot of nighttime thinking. You find it's hard to speak about how you feel. You must speak from the heart and let it all out so you can come out to the light.

You can do this; you just need to believe in yourself. You might need to get some professional help; you will be surprised at how you will feel talking to someone and letting it all out. There is always light at the end of the tunnel, you just can't see it. There is no time like the present – let someone know how you are feeling so you can have the life you desire.

Affirmation: *I allow myself to speak about how I am truly feeling.*

108. SPIDER – *Detail*

I have come to you today to say, The spider is coming in today, and it's all about getting the details right. You need balance in all areas of your life now. You are being pulled in all different directions, but you must come back to centre, and see what direction is best for you. There is a lot of chaos around you, and you can't seem to see what direction is right for you. You must look at each one in more detail before you make any more moves.

You need time to make this decision; take stock of your life, and don't move until you look at all your options. Only then will you know what decision to make. This is a time of looking in great detail at what is working and what is not. You will know when and where to move to when you look at your life with great attention to detail.

Affirmation: *I look at my life with great attention to detail before I make my next move forward.*

109. ARCTIC FOX – *Tricky Situation*

I have come to you today to say, The fox has come to you to say it's all about your physical and mental awareness, seeing through deception, and finding your way around the tricky situation.

The fox is telling you to be aware of what is going on around you. You need to be able to move quickly, as there is someone around you who is being deceitful – be aware of it and take yourself out of this situation before it's too late.

There is a lesson to be learnt from this; do not put your trust in everyone, as not everyone has your best interests at heart. You can be too trusting with others; this is not the first time this has happened to you. Stop giving your trust away so easily.

You must distance yourself from this person before they hurt you badly; your lesson is not to be so trusting the next time.

Affirmation: *I turn my lesson into a blessing.*

110. RED STAG – *Masculine Side*

I have come to you today to say, You are running on your masculine side; whether you are female or male, it's all about control, money, career and ego.

There is too much masculinity going on in your life. You must bring in more of your feminine side. There is also a deep side of you that not a lot of people see; you have a hard exterior, and you don't let people see the soft side of you. You only show what you want people to see.

There is a very soft, loving side of you that you only show to a few people. You find it hard to let people in, and you find it hard to trust. It's OK to let people see the real you, and it's OK to trust them as well. Start by loving yourself and seeing the loving side of yourself. Allow the feminine side to be unleashed; as you do this, all areas of your life will be affected.

Affirmation: *I allow my feminine side to unleash and bring balance to my life.*

111. WOLF – *Support from Your Pack*

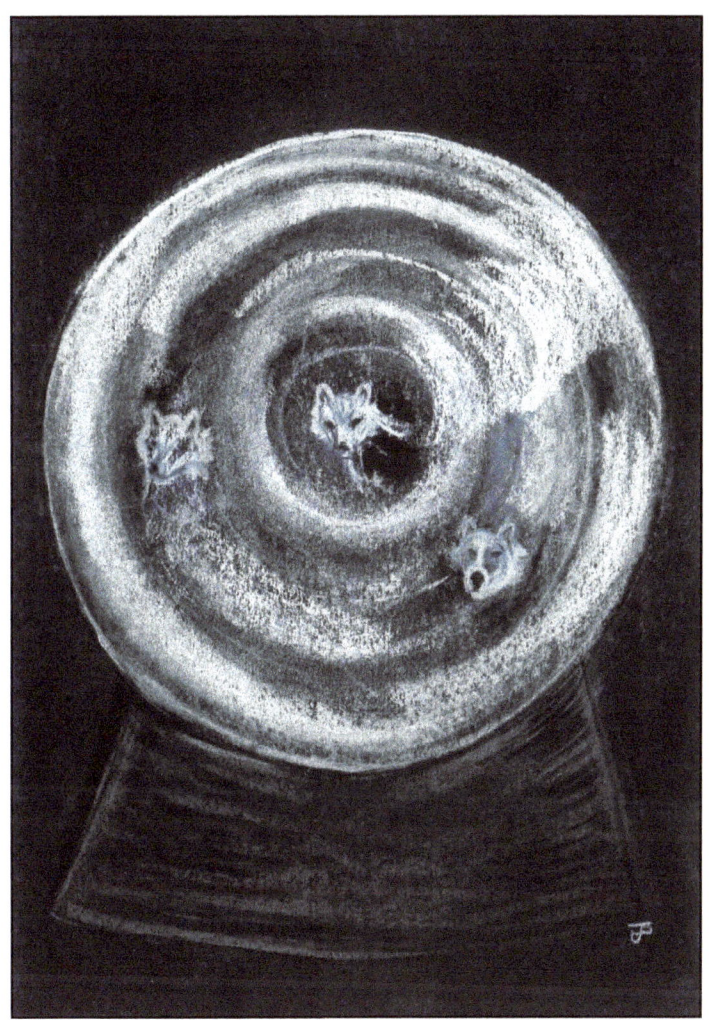

I have come to you today say you are very well supported and protected, and you are very psychic. I am around you all the time.

You need to find your pack to help you along with your spiritual growth. This group of like-minded people will help you along your path. You will be able to talk with ease about what is going on with you, and they will understand and advise you. You will be more at ease on your path as you will get the support that you need from your pack.

I will help you develop your gifts; I will protect you and your loved ones as you open up more of your gifts and allow your inner light to shine.

You are a very deep person who hides a lot, but not anymore. It's time to unleash your true self and allow your pack to support you as you go along your spiritual path. No more holding yourself back.

Affirmation: *I accept support from my pack as I go along my soul's path.*

112. CROW – *Life's Magic*

I have come to you today to help you with your spiritual development, power of insight, transformation, and connection with life's magic. I will help you connect with all aspects of yourself.

I am close, reminding you there is magic all around you that you can't see; you must open up to it more, as this will help you along your spiritual path. The more you open up, the more you will see, hear, and feel. You must believe in yourself, and that you have the capability to see the magic all around you. Don't let fear stand in your way.

Call on me to help you. I am around you all the time. When you feel the fear kicking in, call on me, feel my presence, and I will help you move the energy of fear so you can move forward with ease. The key to this is to trust in your guides and, of course, yourself. Allow your whole self to shine through.

Affirmation: *I see the magic within and all around me.*

113. COW – *Generosity*

I have come to you today to show you how generous you have been and always are to others. You even give when you don't have enough for yourself – this is both a good thing and a bad thing.

Sometimes you over-give, and by over-giving, you bring yourself out of balance. You are not very good at receiving at all, and this has to change to bring your life into balance.

This is your time to break this habit that you have had most of your life. I am not saying to stop giving – I am saying not to over-give. When it comes to receiving, you can get quite embarrassed about it, and you don't feel worthy of receiving anything nice. Sit with yourself and think of the very first time that you didn't feel worthy of receiving; clear the emotion and release it – when you do this, it will start getting easier to receive. It may take a few times going into the energy to fully release it, so be gentle with yourself as you never know what is hidden underneath the energy of unworthiness.

Affirmation: *I am worthy to receive now.*

114. SHEEP – *Unworthy*

I have come to you today to ask you how you are really feeling. Be honest with yourself: you are feeling unworthy. You have been feeling fear, powerlessness and unworthiness. Stop putting yourself last in your life.

You're in a tricky situation in your life, and you need to stop blaming yourself for this. It's time to work out how you are going to get out of this. You need to work out what you want and what you don't want.

You must change your thoughts around this and stop blaming yourself. When you do this, you will be able to move forward from this. Don't let fear or 'what ifs' hold you back. Most importantly, you are worthy of a happy, loving, peaceful life. So, no time like the present – look, see, and change. Only you can make the changes you want. Believe in yourself, no holding back.

Affirmation: *I am worthy of a beautiful life.*

115. BADGER – *Walk Your Own Path*

I have come to you today to say you must walk your own path, at your own pace. You have all the right tools in your bag for whatever challenges you have in your life.

Stop trusting other people and stop looking behind you; you can be very resourceful, and you can sort your own problems out. You can get confused and out of sorts when you start listening to others.

You must keep your feet firmly on the ground, and then you will know what to do and what is important for you, not others.

For you to be successful in your life, you must stop letting others influence you as they think they know best, but in fact, you are the only one who can make the choices for you. It's time to walk your own path and do it with ease.

Affirmation: *I walk my own path with ease.*

116. ROBIN – *Christ Consciousness Energy*

I have come to you today to remind you that you have Christ consciousness energy running through you. You have a special gift that needs to be brought forward; there is no more hiding this gift – you may be a healer, an intuitive.

You can put this gift to good use, but only if you believe in yourself. You have the ability to help others change their lives for the better. This gift has been given to you by Christ to ease others' pain and suffering.

Allow yourself to remove all the self-doubt, fear, and anxiety. You must let go of what other people will think of you and not let this hold you back. If we were to think about what others think, then there would be a world full of people not allowing themselves to move forward. Unleash this energy that is being given to you and allow yourself to take your rightful place on this Earth. The first step is always the hardest, so no holding yourself back; take the step and let your heart and soul sing, doing what you do best: helping others.

Affirmation: *I unleash my true gifts now.*

117. EAGLE – *Time to Take Flight*

I have come to you today to ask you the question, 'Do you need to fly? Do you have the courage to take flight?'

I am asking you to go deep inside yourself and see what you truly want in life. What can you do to get it? Be honest with yourself.

When you do this and get the answer, start taking action and stop making excuses for yourself. You have the strength and courage to go after what you want; you have a tendency to put obstacles in your way. You can be your own worst enemy at times. Let go of all this old energy that you have held on to for years.

Make your mind up, once and for all, and go for it. I can bring you to new heights, a life you can only imagine, if you let me. You must trust and follow every bit of guidance I give you without fail, and you will have that life you are dreaming of. It all comes down to how much you really want it and if you are going to be the pilot of your own life as you take flight.

Affirmation: *I am ready to take flight and fly my own path.*

118. BLACKBIRD – *Mediumship/Clairvoyant*

I have come to you today to let you know that you have a natural ability to connect with the spirit realm. You may know this already, or you are just starting to pick up on the signs now.

You had this ability as a child, but you shut it down through fear; there is nothing to fear as they are only your loved ones. They are trying to connect with you to give you messages and support from the other side.

To develop these gifts, look for a mentor, and they will show you how to protect yourself, and how to open up and close yourself down, as these are very important tools to have. It will come easily to you, so don't let that fear stand in your way. Be like me, the blackbird, and bring the message forward from your loved ones.

Affirmation: *I open myself up to my natural abilities to speak to spirit.*

119. WEASEL – *Silence*

I have come to you today to bring you the silence that you crave so much. Your head is always overthinking, and you have so much going on in your life.

Make time for yourself, for you, some alone time; sit with what is really going on, what are you missing, what signs are you not seeing. You need this time of silence to breathe, get some much-needed rest, and recharge your batteries. You are always running around; you are not giving yourself a minute, you're always on the move. No more: take this time to sit, go within, and allow yourself to just be.

This is a warning sign to slow down; if you don't, spirit has a way of slowing you down if you don't listen. So, take the time off, sit with a book, stay in bed late, watch TV – just chill, do the things that will give you the rest you need, and let go of the guilt. You have earned this rest.

Affirmation: *I give myself permission to rest.*

120. WHITE BUFFALO – *Choose Peace*

I have come to you today to say choose peace over chaos. You have been looking for peace in your life for some time now; you can have this peace you so desire.

You must make peace with yourself first and let go of the hurt and guilt and the dramas that you are holding on to.

You can get so involved in drama that you let it take over your life. You have come to a point in your life where you are asking yourself why you're surrounded by so much drama, and you want a peaceful life so much.

You are creating this on some level, so when you feel yourself stepping into the drama, ask yourself if you really want this. Step back and choose peace over chaos – it can be that simple if you want it to be. You can have the option to get involved, but you don't need to fully step into it. Now that you are aware of what you are doing, you can change the outcome. It's up to you to choose peace over chaos.

Affirmation: *I allow peace to descend into my life.*

121. ELEPHANT – *Goddess*

I have come to you today to ask you to unleash your divine goddess within you and let go.

I am asking you to allow your true beauty, love, and sexuality to unleash and allow it to unfold in all areas of your life. When you fully embrace your divine feminine qualities, you will see your life change for the better. You have been suppressing this for far too long. You have a very compassionate side to you; when you allow others to see this side of you, they see the true essence of you.

The divine goddess is compassionate, loving, sexual, and a warrior. You have all these qualities within you – you just can't see them. Allow me to help you unleash them, express who you truly are, and embrace your true self. This is your time to fully step out and be seen for the true divine goddess that you are.

Affirmation: *I unleash my divine goddess within me now.*

122. INDIAN TIGER – *Inner Warrior*

I have come to you today to help you awaken your inner warrior. This side of you has been asleep for far too long; you have been going through life with no real action.

Now is your time to awaken your inner warrior as you want more out of life. Are you feeling fed up, just going along with things for the sake of it, not really knowing where or what you want, always in the background?

Not anymore – there is a warrior within you looking to get out and be the person you have been dreaming of, the person who goes for what they want in life and doesn't let anything or anyone get in their way. The person who has great belief in themselves and lets the world see who they truly are. Call on me to help guide you, let go of the block, and unlock your inner warrior.

Affirmation: *I unleash my inner warrior now.*

123. WHITE RHINO – *Stability*

I have come to you today to help you bring the stability into your life that you have been seeking for a while.

It seems like every time you try to get stable, it fails – but not anymore. You have been going about it the wrong way. You are not putting the proper actions in place, but you're expecting the results and wondering why it's not happening.

You must look at why there is no stability and see where and what needs to change. Make a plan of action, and bring these changes in one by one, slowly. As you do this, it will bring the changes and also the stability you want.

Call on me to help and guide you through these changes and start living the life you have been dreaming of for so long.

Affirmation: *I bring stability into all areas of my life.*

124. LADYBIRD – *Dare*

I have come today to ask you, 'Do you dare to follow your dreams?' Are you that person that goes for their dreams no matter what? Or are you the person who wishes they did?

You know what you have to do to get to your dream – so what is stopping you? What are you afraid of? The choice to follow your dreams is yours, not anyone else's.

Stop making excuses; start giving yourself daily tasks and take action each day. Small steps are your way forward at the moment. When you are feeling the fear, acknowledge it and still take the action – this is your only way forward, and you are not allowing fear to win.

Ask yourself if you dare to follow your dreams and take action; you have the ability to create the life you are dreaming of. Call on me to help you create this and follow your dreams. Dreams do come true when we believe in ourselves.

Affirmation: *I dare to follow my dreams now.*

125. HAMSTER – *Round and Round*

I have come to you today because you are like me, on the hamster wheel, going round and round, and you can't seem to get out of it.

You want to change things in your life, but don't seem to know where to start. That's OK. The first thing you need to do is decide what you want to change and then take the action that will change it.

The first step to change is knowing that you want to change, then the rest will fall into place. Don't be so hard on yourself; we can all get stuck from time to time – the main thing is you know and see that you want to change. Be gentle with yourself as you go through this. Let go of self-judgement and be that person you want to be.

Affirmation: *I see, and I am willing to make the changes to move forward.*

126. RAT – *Big Things*

I have come to you today to tell you big things are coming into your life. Yes, big things.

This may be in the form of winning money, a new job, a promotion, an exciting new way of living, or even that move you have been dreaming of.

This is a life changer; you have been asking for change for a while now, you have set your sights high, and it's about to pay off. You have great belief in yourself; you can do anything you put your mind to – there is no stopping you.

Even when it didn't look like it was going to work out in your favour, you never gave up. Give yourself a pat on the back. Well done you, you never gave up.

Now is the time to sit back and enjoy your reward, you have done this! You have manifested the life of your dreams!

Affirmation: *I am a winner in life.*

127. PIG – *Sniffing*

I have come to you today to say you are very good at sniffing out new opportunities, and you are always making them work out in your favour.

You have the ability to always be in the right place at the right time. And opportunities just land in your lap. This is a great way to be in life; life never gets dull. There is a dream opportunity coming your way soon. This is something that you have been looking for, for some time now.

Do what you do best, sniff around, and keep on the lookout so this does not pass you by, as this is a once-in-a-lifetime offer, and it will not present itself to you again. Don't hesitate when it presents itself to you; go for it and ask questions later. Call on me to help you see the opportunity and go for gold. Yes, you can have it all and more.

Affirmation: *I can have it all and more.*

128. HEN – *Time*

I have come to you today to say you are always running out of time. You always seem to be running around like a headless chicken with no time at all for the good things in life.

When was the last time you stopped and did something nice or had some fun? You are not doing yourself any favours by running around like this. The only thing that will happen is you will become ill – that is our way of slowing you down, as you are not listening to us.

Take some time out for yourself; just sit, catch up with family and friends, go out, have some fun. Most of all, catch up with yourself and make that much-needed time for yourself. The most important person in your life is you. I hear you say, 'That's selfish!' but it's not – it's just looking after yourself. Call on me, and I will help you make that much-needed time for you and for fun.

Affirmation: *I make time to look after myself and have some fun now.*

129. PEACOCK – *Third Eye*

I have come to you today to say it's all about the third eye – you need to open it fully to see all around you.

You must trust in your own intuition; just go with whatever you are getting. I will open my feathers when I trust in myself, so you must do this for yourself to open your third eye fully. Walk away from fear as you are a very capable person; you just must believe in yourself. Call on me to help you trust and grow in your intuition.

As your third eye opens wide like the peacock's feathers, trust and believe in the information you are receiving. You are here as a channel to the spirit world, to tell their stories, commute and pass on their messages to a loved one. Be like me: open up, strut, and believe in yourself.

Affirmation: *I trust myself; I believe in myself.*

130. DOLPHIN – *Manifest*

I have come to you today to let you know you have the ability to manifest the life you have been dreaming of.

You are a great manifester – you are manifesting on a daily basis. You must be very careful about what you are thinking about and keep your thoughts positive. You don't want to manifest what you don't want in your life.

Keep your thoughts clear and positive. Start on something small first; think of what you want, put your manifesting skills to work, and see how fast you can manifest it. Then start on the bigger things you want, and you will have your dreams in no time.

You must keep yourself grounded and positive at all times for this to work. Call on me: I will help you ground and be positive to manifest your dreams.

Affirmation: *I am grounded and positive, and I manifest my dreams.*

131. WHALE – *Bridge the Gap*

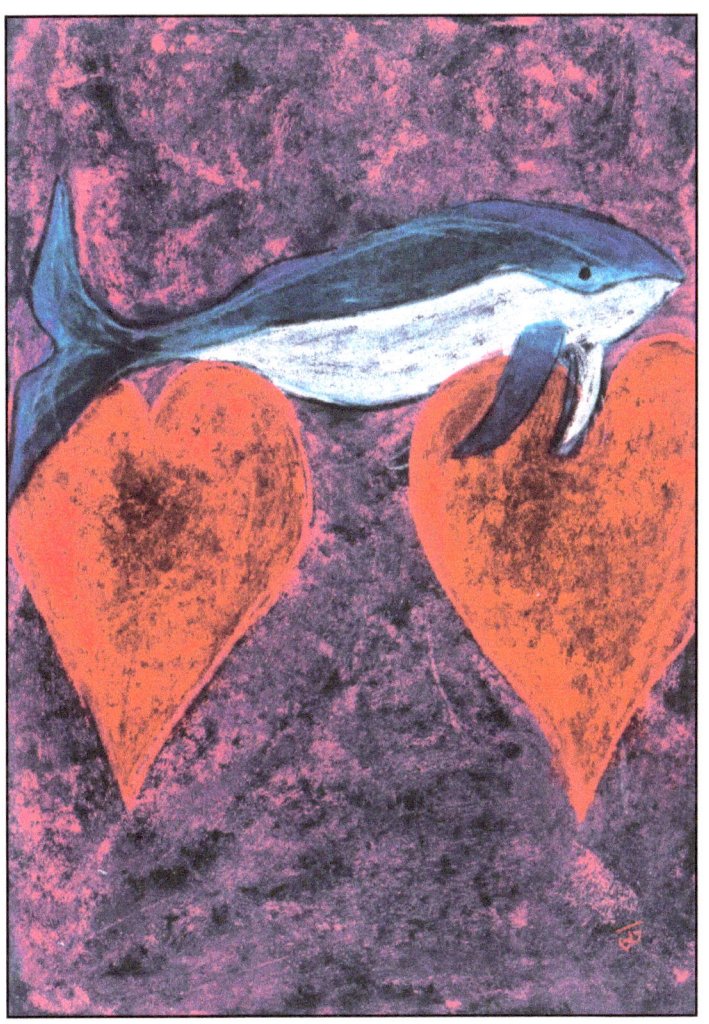

I have come to you today to help you bridge the gap between you and a loved one.

You have a very strong connection between you and a loved one, but at times you seem to feel you are not on the same level. Call on me to help you bridge this gap. Sit and remember what you like doing together. Make an effort to spend more time together doing what you love to do. This will strengthen your relationship and bring you closer.

You must let go of your insecurities and allow your relationship to heal. It's OK not to be on the same level; we all like different things in life, but the most important thing in your relationship is your love for one another. All relationships go through rough patches. Open up and tell the other person how you are feeling, as they are probably feeling this way as well. Call on me to help you find the solutions to bridge the gap.

Affirmation: *I am in a happy, healthy relationship now.*

132. SHARK – *Environment*

I have come to you today to say you should be doing more for the environment.

Are you doing enough for the environment, or are you letting others do it for you? You must look at the ways in your life that you can help the environment.

Are using chemicals to clean, wasting water daily, not recycling, or wasting paper? There are so many ways that you can help the environment on a daily basis. Just look at what you are doing daily.

You can change these habits, and when you do, you will feel so much better for it as you will be doing your bit to help and save Mother Earth for further generations.

Affirmation: *I do my bit to help save Mother Earth.*

133. OCTOPUS – *Creativity*

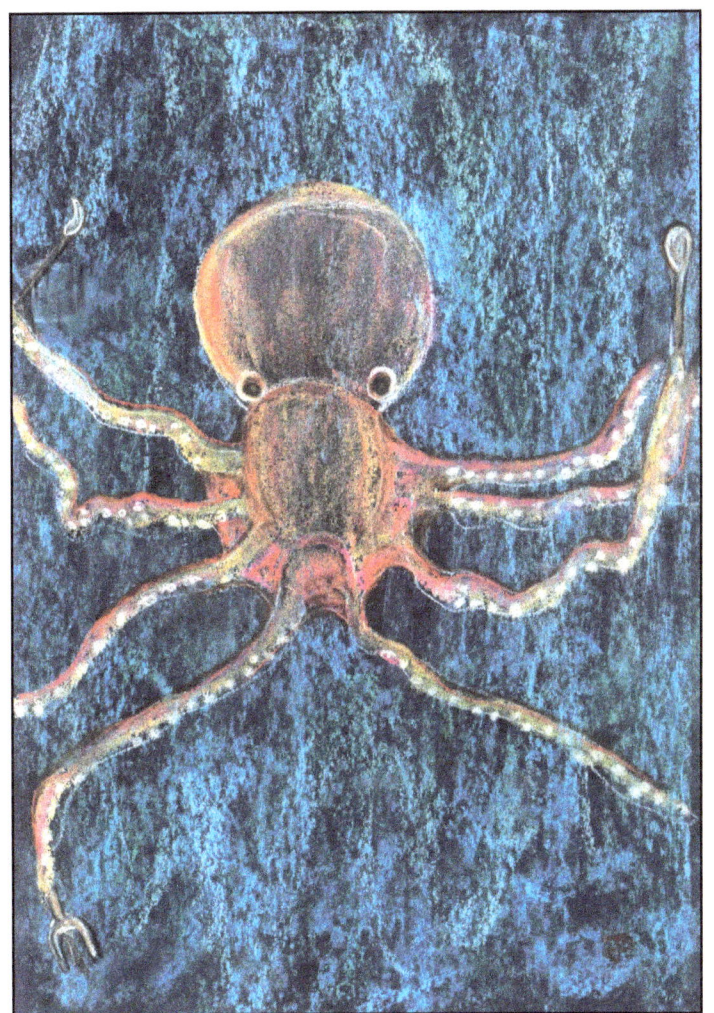

I have come to you today to say it's time to unleash your creativity.

It's time to unlock your creativity, as there is so much you can do. You may be saying, 'I am not creative; I can't draw.' But you don't need to be an artist to be creative – you can do anything you put your mind to.

Your creative side could be sewing, knitting, baking, design, or gardening. These are all ways to create. When you are creative, you flow, and it comes so naturally to you. It brings balance into your life, and you start to see things differently.

Think of something creative you can do, allow yourself the time and space to do it, and see how it uplifts your mood. Then the flow and balance come in naturally. You will be surprised how easy it can be; enjoy the flow and balance within.

Affirmation: *I allow my creativity to flow.*

134. SEA HORSE – *Inspire*

I have come to you today to say you can inspire others along their path.

You have a gift that helps others to see their true self; you are a very trustworthy person and care deeply. A lot of people look to you for advice.

You seem to attract people when they need help. You always help them, no matter what, and you go out of your way to help. You always inspire them with your words of wisdom. You have helped a lot of people in different situations move forward in their lives. You always know what to say and do.

You inspire others to see how they can change their lives and do the best for themselves; you make them feel good about themselves and you see the best qualities in them. Allow yourself to see these amazing qualities you have and see the good you do with others; you are an inspiration – keep up the good work.

Affirmation: *I inspire others to be themselves.*

135. GOAT – *Seeing the World*

I have come to you today to ask how you are viewing the world.

Are you getting caught up in all the negativity of the media? Is this energy affecting you? You must stop, step back, and see what is really going on for yourself. We all view things differently, but you are allowing all this to get to you; it is causing you to go into fear and overwhelm, and your anxiety levels are sky high.

Turn off the media, TV, Facebook, etc., as this is causing your energy level to dip. Yes, we do need to know what is going on in the world, but not to watch or listen 24/7. Call on me to help you clear this negative energy out of your mind, body, and soul, and help you bring the positive back into your life. You will feel so much better when you step out of the drama of the media and step back into your life and bring back positive energy.

Affirmation: *I see the world through my own eyes.*

136. SNAKE – *Kundalini*

I have come to you today to let you know that your kundalini energy is ready to rise. You may have gone through this before; if so, this is another awakening for you, and you are ready to go to the next level of concussions. Feel the kundalini energy in the base of your spine – it's coiled like a snake.

As you allow this to rise, you will feel this energy move from the base of your spine, like the snake, all the way up through your chakra system, awakening and balancing each chakra along the way, letting go of what no longer serves you. This is your awakening to your next journey along your soul's path. Call on me to help clear and remove any fear in your way.

Affirmation: *I allow myself to take the next step along my soul's journey.*

137. MONKEY – *See!*

I have come to you today to say, 'Monkey see, monkey do!' You are following a lot of different people and doing what they say, hanging on their every word, jumping from one spiritual practice to another, and you are wondering why you are a bit stuck.

You don't have to follow what others say. You must listen to yourself because what works for them might not work for you, because we all have our own way of doing things. Stop jumping from one thing to another; stick with one thing and practice this for a least two months, then see if it worked or if you need to tweak it slightly. You will know, yourself, what to do.

You will know deep down if something works for you or not – you just need to listen and trust in yourself. It's time to see your uniqueness and let it shine and shine bright.

Affirmation: *I allow myself to see me.*

138. GORILLA – *Vocalise*

I have come to you today to say you must vocalise yourself in a different way to be heard. You have taken to shouting when you are not being heard, but when this happens, others just shut down and switch off, which is not good for you, as it makes you worse.

You feel like nobody is listening to you or what you are saying, or that it's falling on deaf ears, and this is why you feel you have to shout for them to listen to you. Well, it's not working, and you are the only one getting upset.

Maybe when they don't listen, walk away from them before you get to the level that you have to shout. You can go from 1 to 10 in half a second and then all hell breaks loose, which does nobody any good. By walking away before this happens, you will approach things much calmer, and then you won't have to shout. You will be heard, and there will be no drama – it's a win-win. Call on me – it helps you to do this – and see the change and effect it will have on you.

Affirmation: *I step out of the drama and into peace.*

139. DEER – *See Yourself*

I have come to you today to ask how you are seeing yourself, or whose eyes you are seeing yourself through.

You have been putting yourself down lately about how you look, act, speak, etc. You are not seeing your true self. If you only saw yourself through the eyes of others and how they see you, you would see yourself very differently.

Look at yourself in the mirror; look deep within your eyes and say to yourself, over and over until you truly believe, 'I love myself; I trust myself, and I believe in myself.' As you do this, it will clear all the excess baggage away; this may take you a good few times before you clear everything. Yes, it can be hard to look in the mirror at oneself and say those words, but no matter how uncomfortable it feels, don't give up – you will get there.

You can change how you feel about yourself by doing this. The effect of this is huge and will change your life for the better, so there is no time like the present – start today.

Affirmation: *I love myself; I trust myself; I believe in myself.*

140. CAMEL – *Hydration*

I have come to you today to say you need to be more hydrated, as your work is draining you of your body fluids; you must drink more water.

I advise you to double your intake of water, as this will help you. You have been feeling a bit off lately, and you can't seem to concentrate for long – this is because you are dehydrated. It's important that you drink as much as you can to hydrate your body. This will bring you back into balance; you will have more energy, strengthen your immune system, and feel so much better.

Be like me and store as much water as you can, and it will keep you full, balanced, and well within yourself.

Affirmation: *I keep myself hydrated.*

141. GIRAFFE – *Visualisation*

I have come to you today to say you must start visualising what you thoroughly want in life; ask yourself that question, and be bold.

It's time to dream big and use your skills to go and get it. If you can visualise it, then it can become a reality. Ask yourself the question and let your imagination do the rest.

When you visualise your dream, don't leave any detail out, not even the smallest one; feel it, smell it, and taste it – use all your senses as you do this. Feel like you already have this, and it's your reality. See it like a movie, and you are the leading role; no holding back your imagination, allow it to run wild, and it will become your reality. Do this on a daily basis and believe it as it will come true. Don't hold yourself back, your dream is waiting to become your reality.

Affirmation: *My dreams become my reality.*

142. LEOPARD – *Motivation*

I have come to you today to say you have lost your motivation; you are just letting life pass you by and can't seem to get yourself going.

Your vibration and energy seem to be very low; you want to get up and go, but you just can't seem to get there. Your energy seems to be depleted. You are letting every small thing get to you and finding it hard to cope, and you are not doing any self-care – this is affecting all areas of your life.

It's time to get up and dust yourself off, call all your energy back from people, places, and situations, cut all the cords that are binding you to them, and ground deeply into Mother Earth. You will feel so much better after you have done this. You must not allow anyone in your energy as they are draining you, and this causes you to feel depleted and have no motivation. It's important that you do this daily, and you will feel your strength, energy, and motivation come back. Call on me to help you regain your strength, and you will be back to your old self sooner than you think.

Affirmation: *I am strong and powerful.*

143. PANDA – *Balance*

I have come to you today to say you need balance in your life.

I am helping you to bring balance, set better boundaries, and bring much-needed balance into your life as an unbalanced life does nobody any good.

When we don't have the proper boundaries in our lives, people can take advantage of our gentle, loving natures, and the only person who benefits is the other person. You have been giving far too much of yourself to others with no return. This has to change. You are always giving, and you are unbalanced; you can find it hard to receive.

This unbalance is affecting your life and it has caused you to become unwell; you seem to be in a bit of a dark place. Now is your time to take your power back and allow yourself to balance the receiving and giving. As you do this, you will find it will have a ripple effect and you will find balance in all areas of your life. It will take time, but remember you can do these small steps to create big results.

Affirmation: *I allow myself balance in all areas of my life now.*

144. WORM – *Healing Insecurities*

I have come to you today to say it's time to heal your insecurities, as they are holding you back on all levels.

You have been telling yourself for too long now that you are not good enough, worthy enough, or clever enough – the list is endless. ENOUGH. Take a good look at yourself in the mirror and ask yourself if this is the life you really want. You know the answer deep down, and it's time to do something about it. Only you can do this, nobody else can do this for you.

Start by seeing the loving person you are, the love you give others, and direct that love to yourself and see the difference that it will make. Say positive affirmations, feeling what you are saying. Small steps make a big difference. Every step towards healing your insecurities brings you closer to loving yourself unconditionally, and when we achieve that, we hold within us inner peace.

Affirmation: *I love myself. (Repeat as often as you can.)*

145. HIPPO – *Suppressed*

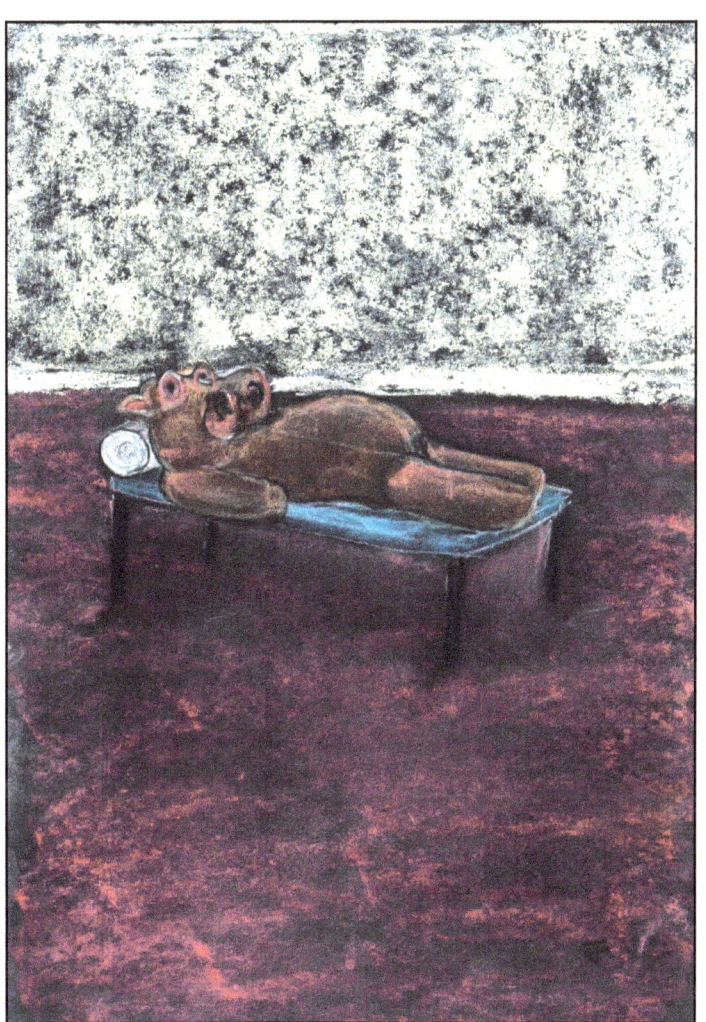

I have come to you today to ask you, what have you suppressed within yourself and why are you holding on to it?

You have a deep emotion suppressed within you; this is blocking you from evolving to the next level on your soul's path.

You may need help from a mentor/healer to unearth this; it could be from a past life or even this lifetime. It is very deep – it has been hiding from you as you were not ready to deal with it until now.

You have done a lot of work on yourself, and you may be thinking, 'Here we go again, more crap to release, more pain.' It only causes pain when we don't surrender. You have a tendency to hold on, but not this time. I will help you let this go with ease and flow, like the way I move through the water. Allow yourself to fully surrender this emotion. Let go and allow yourself to go to your next level of consciousness.

Affirmation: *I surrender with ease and grace now.*

146. PARROT – *Ask for Help*

I have come today to say it's OK to ask others for help.

You would rather go through what you are going through and not ask for help or even talk about it to anyone. You hold it all in, but this is not doing you any good at all; it is causing you a lot of stress. You must start asking others for help and talk about how you are feeling instead of holding it all in. Sit down with a friend whom you trust and let it all out; you will be surprised by how supportive they are, and they might be able to help you with a solution.

We all need support from others from time to time. We can't do it all by ourselves. It's OK to trust others. You have been hurt in the past when you put your trust in someone else; you must let this go – it's in the past, so leave it there. Enough is enough; you need the support and help now, so just ask – it's not too late. Call on me to help you ask and get the help that you need.

Affirmation: *I receive the help and support that I need now.*

147. MEERKAT – *Anger*

I have come to you today to ask you why you are holding on to so much anger.

You need to release the anger you are holding onto before you let it loose on the wrong person. You are like a pressure cooker about to explode.

This anger is very deep within you, bubbling away. Sit with yourself and forgive yourself or who or what caused you to be this angry, as it's doing you no good holding onto it.

Release it in any way that feels right for you. You may feel like crying, screaming, punching a pillow, or banging a tea towel on the table – release it in a safe way, and let it all go. Once you have done this, you will feel so much better, although you may have to do this a few times to fully release all that you are holding onto. When we forgive, we heal on so many levels, and this allows us to move forward.

Affirmation: *I let go of the anger and free myself now.*

148. PANDA – *Honour Yourself*

I have come to you today to tell you to honour yourself. You are a very sensitive person, and you have been like this all your life. You seem to think it's not a good way to be, but you are wrong. You are very sensitive to other people's emotions, and you seem to pick them up without knowing you are doing so; you must shield yourself from this. You are an empath, and you feel things on a very deep level. Sometimes you feel misunderstood and overwhelmed. When this happens, you are taking on too much of other people's emotions.

You must clear your energy on a very deep level; ground and make sure nobody else is in your energy. Take a deep breath in and allow yourself to ground deep into Mother Earth. Call back all your energy, ask for anyone in your energy to be released, and ask for anything that is deeply hidden to be removed. Place a bubble of love, light, and protection around you as a shield. Remember to do this daily and you will feel better as you won't be taking on so much of other people's energy. Also, connect with nature as this will keep you grounded.

Affirmation: *I honour my sensitivity.*

149. ZEBRA – *Compromise*

I have come to you today to ask you why you are compromising yourself and your values; be 100% honest with yourself before it's too late.

You seem to be letting someone else project their values onto you. You have let this person take over to some degree and you are hanging on their every word. Step back from this person and ask yourself if their values are your values. Be honest, as you are compromising yourself.

You are a much better person than this, and you have very high values; you don't normally compromise or lower your standards. Stop letting others control you, and take back control of your own life and values. Call on me to give you the strength to do this and start living your life fully again.

Affirmation: *I value myself always.*

150. HEDGEHOG – *Unleash Yourself*

I have come to you today to unleash yourself and become the person you want to be. Stop holding yourself back and allow the true you to emerge from the shield of armour you have placed around you. This shield does not serve you any longer, so it's time to drop it. Allow yourself to be seen for the loving person that you are; there is no more hiding the real you.

It's time you come out from behind the shield – it's stopping you from moving forward, finding love, and being happy. It's time to take that chance on love. You won't know how it feels if you don't take that chance and let that person in; you will be surprised at how good it will feel. Open your heart and let all the past hurts go – leave them in the past where they belong. Let your new love in and have the happiness you so desire. This is your time to find the love you have been dreaming of.

Affirmation: *I drop my shield, and I allow love in.*

151. OWL – *End of a Cycle*

I have come to you today to let you know you are coming to an end of a cycle within your life; it's a time to start fresh.

You may have been feeling that you want to change something in your life and try something new; this is the right time to do this. You are letting go of all the old and it's clearing your energy to bring in something new.

You will start to have new ideas about what you want to do. Don't rush into anything; be sure this is what you really want, and then go for it.

There is also a situation coming to an end for you. You have been praying for this, and your prayers are about to be answered. The cycle will be done, and the lesson learnt. It will be like an ending and then a beginning. Allow yourself to let all the old energy go and make room for the new – call on me to help you get through this.

Affirmation: *I let go of the old to make way for the new.*

152. BEAR – *Leadership*

I have come to you today to say it's time to take your leadership role in life. You have great leadership qualities, but you are not using them to your advantage. You are allowing yourself to be overlooked. You have the drive, communication skills, confidence, and commitment to be the leader you are meant to be.

Look at the qualities you have and use them to your advantage; set a good example for others. You have a positive attitude, you are a good communicator, and you give and receive respect. Put all these qualities into your business and lead yourself on the path of success. You can't fail, so go for it. You have nothing to lose; believe and trust in yourself.

Affirmation: *I act and communicate like a leader.*

153. POLAR BEAR – *Quiet Time*

I have come to you today to say there is a need for you to have some quiet time. You must take yourself out of all the hustle and bustle of the world.

You are being guided to take a short break to spend some time reconnecting with yourself. Allow yourself to unwind. Life has taken you over, and you just can't seem to get yourself or your thoughts to gather or concentrate on anything at all. We can get so caught up in all that is going on that we forget about ourselves; we can put our own best interests on the back burner.

You are tired, fed up with it all, and you are craving quiet time. Book that much-needed rest, and when you do, switch off your phone, log out of social media and disconnect from the world. Go for long walks, have a lie-in, do only what you want to do. As you do this, you will feel yourself coming back and you will feel more like yourself. Go ahead – book and take that much-needed rest; you deserve it.

Affirmation: *I allow myself to retreat within myself.*

154. SEA LION – *Focus*

I have come to you today to ask you what you are focusing on, because you are not focusing on what you should be.

For you to bring in what you want, you must focus on it. You must let your creative juices flow and your imagination explode, no holding back. You have a very strong imagination; you are just not allowing yourself to use it to your advantage.

You seem to think that imagination is for children, but you are very wrong. When we let our imagination loose, we see, feel, and sense our dreams. Once we do this, then we can bring our dreams to our reality. Let go of the negative thoughts around your imagination and set yourself free. Focus on what you want, imagine it and allow the dream to become your reality. You must do this on a daily basis and then follow the guidance. Dream big, and let your imagination run wild.

Affirmation: *I allow my imagination to run wild.*

155. ANTELOPE – *Happening Quickly*

I have come today to say, hold on tight: it's all about to happen and quickly.

You feel like there is something brewing, but you don't know what it is. You can feel the energy of excitement around you, and it is making you feel a bit on edge. There is no need to worry; all that is coming to you is for your own good. You have been asking for change for a while now, and it's about to happen.

New doors are opening up for you; you are going to get that once-in-a-lifetime offer, so stop pushing, and allow it to flow. When we push, we push it away from us, so allow these changes to come in with ease, and get out of your own way. I can come in to help in that new relationship. New job, new ideas, and more. This change is going to happen quickly, so be on your guard and enjoy every bit of it as you have been through a rough couple of months. Things are on the up.

Affirmation: *I step through the door of change with ease.*

156. CHAMELEON – *Blending into the Background*

I have come to you today to say stop blending into the background. Allow yourself to be seen.

You have a bad habit of not wanting to be seen; you don't like to be put in the spotlight. When you are around others, you hold yourself back, try not to be seen, and will only give your opinion when you are asked to. You have done this most of your life, but not anymore.

This is your time to stand out from the crowd, to be seen for who you truly are; there is no point in trying to hide anymore. You have a lot to say and do, so step out, let the world see the true you, no more hiding. There is a whole new world waiting on you, you just need to allow yourself to go out and get it. No more holding back – it's time to take hold of your life.

Affirmation: *I allow the world to see me.*

157. SLOTH – *Carefree*

I have come to you today to say it's time to let your carefree side out. You used to live a very carefree life, but not anymore.

You have let responsibilities bring you down. You have got yourself into a very awkward situation and can't seem to see the way out, or someone is holding you there. You must let it all go. Let go of the control or step out of the control. You know you have taken on too much. It has become hard, so it's time to get out now before you get too deep in, before it's too late and you get hurt.

You are being guided by me to help you see what is truly going on. Stop, look, and be honest with yourself. Do you really want this in your life, or do you want that carefree life that you used to have? If so, this is your time to reclaim the life that you want, make a clean break, and set yourself free. You are the only one that can do this.

Affirmation: *I set myself free to be carefree now.*

158. DUCK – *Reconnection*

I have come to you today to say it's time to reconnect with family or an old friend.

This person is coming back into your life from your past; those people may have hurt you, but you have held on to the hurt for a long time. This may be through a chance meeting, social media, a call, or text. It will bring up a lot of the old painful memories and the hurt that you have hidden for a long time. This is happening for a reason, as this has stopped you from moving forward along your path. It is time to release this old energy.

You are being asked to forgive yourself and this person. Allow both of you to heal and let it go, as it no longer serves either of you. It's time to move forward from the pain and move into love; as you do this, you set yourself free to move forward along your path. Yes, it can be hard looking back and revisiting the old past hurts, so call on me to help you do this.

Affirmation: *I forgive and allow myself to move forward with ease.*

159. DONKEY – *Deep Truth*

I have come to you today to say it's time for you to unlock your truth and inspire yourself and others

There is a deep truth within you wanting to be unlocked. You are here at this time to inspire others and allow them to look within to see their true selves. You know you are about to embark on your soul's mission, but you are holding yourself back on some level; you may be thinking that you are not, but you are.

We all do it from time to time, so don't get too caught up in it. It is your time to let go and go deep within every level, every layer of yourself. Yes, it will be hard, but you are ready for it, and you are much stronger than you think. Call me to help you peel back the layers. Don't let fear hold your truth back. You have come here to fulfil your soul's mission and take your rightful place on this Earth, to help and inspire others to unlock their true selves.

Affirmation: *I help and inspire others to unlock their true selves.*

160. CRAB – *New Direction*

I have come to you today to let you know there is a new direction on your spiritual journey about to open up to you.

You are being shown a new direction along your journey; it will unfold within the next few weeks. It is something that you have great interest in, and you are being shown this new direction as it will bring you closer to your dreams.

You have a lot of gifts that will be revealed to you along this journey. They will be your tools, and you will use these tools to help yourself and your clients. When a problem presents itself, you will go into your spiritual tool bag and pull the tool you need to help yourself or your client. This new direction will open you up to a new way of being. Let go of the old and embrace your new way of being.

Affirmation: *I embrace the new.*

161. BEE – *Hard Working*

I have come to you today to say you are working too hard; you are so caught up in your work that you are letting life pass you by.

There is a need to get your work and family life in balance. You must work but not at the expense of your family life. You feel you need to provide for everyone and give them the good things in life, but what they really need is you.

When was the last time that you had some good old-fashioned fun, laughed your head off, and let go of the worry and stress? It's like you just can't seem to switch off. You're always thinking about the next project, the next client, and whatever has to be done. Do yourself a favour: stop and bring that much-needed balance into all areas of your life.

Release the need to provide for everyone and go have some fun. Let your hair down and bring that much-needed happiness and balance into your life; you will feel much better within yourself.

Affirmation: *I am a magnet for fun times.*

162. WASP – *Development*

I have come to you today to say it's time for you to develop your spiritual skills more to expand your knowledge.

You are going to embark on a new journey and develop your skills on a deeper level. You are about to remember and reawaken the gifts that have been hidden from you until now, as you were not ready for them – but you are now.

You might need the help of a mentor or a healer to help you go within on a very deep level, to let go of all old untruths that are no longer serving you. You may find it hard at times. When you are feeling this way, remind yourself of how far you have come and how well you are doing. Never give up as you never know what tomorrow will bring. Allow yourself to develop and expand to your next level of consciousness.

Affirmation: *I never give up.*

163. FLY – *Persistent*

I have come to you today to say it's time to be persistent in what you are doing and commit 100% to your goals.

You are not going to get to where you want by doing it willy-nilly and not putting your heart into it. You seem to be jumping from one thing to another and hoping something will work to bring your dream to you.

Stop what you are doing now, as it is not working. Sit down and make a list of what action you should be taking. Do this on a daily basis, one step at a time, as Rome wasn't built in a day. Every step brings you closer. The key to fulfilling your dreams is persistence; even if you don't feel like doing it, you must, no matter what. This persistence will bring you your dreams and allow you to have the life that you have been dreaming of. No holding yourself back – yes, you can do it.

Affirmation: *I persist, and I will succeed.*

164. BUTTERFLY – *Take your Time*

I have come to you today to say slow down and take your time. Like the caterpillar, you must give yourself time to go through a metamorphosis and allow yourself to change.

You have been doing so much inner work; now is the time for you to let it all integrate. You have let so many old beliefs and patterns go, and you are becoming your true self.

You are feeling tired, with low energy, a bit out of sorts, and can't seem to understand what is going on. You need to take it easy like the caterpillar, go into the metamorphosis stage, and allow your body to integrate all the new energy that has come in for you. Stop being so hard on yourself, take the much-needed time to rest, and allow your true divine self – your 'I am' presence – to emerge.

Affirmation: *I give myself permission to integrate all that I am.*

165. PENGUIN – *Chaos*

I have come to you today to say that the chaos you feel around you is about to be over.

You are going through a chaotic time at the moment. That's OK, as there is order coming in through the chaos. It is essential that you keep moving forward with your plans and dreams and see the significance in the small things unfolding. Don't dismiss the little things that are happening, as they bring through great changes. Try not to become disillusioned; there is light at the end of the tunnel, you just can't see it yet.

Hang in there – it will soon be over. The chaotic time is happening for a reason; it is showing you what you don't want. Just before a breakthrough happens, our world around us becomes chaotic, so hold on as you go through this; it will all work out in the end. Call on me to help you see the light at the end of the tunnel.

Affirmation: *I embrace the chaos.*

166. OSTRICH – *Declutter*

I have come to you today to say there is a need to declutter your mind, body, and home of stagnant energy.

There is a need to go through every inch of your home, declutter, and get rid of the old – from books to clothes, as everything has energy. When you hold to things, you hold on to the old energy, and that's not good for anyone.

The best way to do this is to set out three piles: rubbish, charity shop, and keep. Keep the special stuff until last; as you do this, you are not only clearing your home, you are clearing yourself as well. When you have finished clearing your belongings, burn some sage, open every window, and set the intention of clearing all old energy out. When you are finished, set the intentions to bring in new energy, then clear your own energy as this allows you to bring in new beginnings. It's time for you to move forward with ease.

Affirmation: *I move forward with ease.*

167. CROCODILE – *Forceful*

I have come to you today to ask what you are being too forceful about. Maybe it's time to be a bit gentler.

You can come across as very forceful at times, and this can intimidate others. Maybe take a look at how you are speaking to others and change your mannerisms.

Some people can be taken aback by the way you can say things, and it comes across the wrong way. Be mindful of the way you speak to them, and be gentler in the way you say it. You can get your point across in a better way; they will take on what you are saying if it comes across in a gentler way. Step back, think, allow what you want to say, let it come from the heart and say it with ease. Be gentle with yourself and allow your gentle side to shine.

Affirmation: *I allow my gentle side to shine.*

168. EMU – *Excellence*

I have come to you today to say you have an air of excellence around you; you are brilliant at what you do.

You don't seem to see this quality within yourself. Your gifts come to you very naturally, and you don't seem to see how amazing your gifts are, how you help and serve others.

You can't seem to take a compliment or praise when it is given to you. You feel embarrassed on some level, and you downplay your achievements. You just don't get how gifted you are and how it has and can help so many people, or how it has transformed their lives. Take the praise when it is given to you and enjoy it, as it is so deserved. You are excellent at what you do.

Affirmation: *I allow myself to see my excellent gifts.*

169. KANGAROO – *Leap of Faith*

I have come to you today to say it's your time to take that leap of faith.

What is holding you back? This is the question you must ask, and be honest with yourself. When we want something so badly, when it comes, we can go into fear, overwhelm, and not feeling good enough.

You have put yourself out there, and you have done all the work to get you this far. So, go for it, take that leap of faith – nothing is holding you back but you. Stop blocking yourself. This is your time; your dreams are about to become your reality, so don't let fear win. Yes, you have the strength to do this one last thing for it all to fall into place, so go ahead, you have nothing to lose.

Affirmation: *I know that it's time to take my leap of faith.*

170. KOALA BEAR – *Mindful*

I have come to you today to say you are a very sweet soul, and you are very mindful of others.

You have such a beautiful quality about you, and you are very gentle. You always put others before yourself. This can be both a strength and a weakness. You don't judge others, and you are very mindful about how that person feels. Sometimes, you can take in their energy, without even knowing you are doing this. This is not good for you.

We can be mindful of others and look out for ourselves as well. We must be our first priority and get the balance right; we can't give to others if we don't look after ourselves. Do yourself a favour and put your self-care practice into place, cut the cords, and protect your energy on a regular basis. You can look after and help others, but you must look after yourself first.

Affirmation: *I put my own needs before others now.*

171. PORCUPINE – *Head On*

I have come to you today to say stop running and face your fears head-on; you must do this to move forward.

Yes, it can be hard to face your fears. You have a tendency to brush them under the carpet, but not anymore. You must look at what is holding you back and why. Go deep within; if you can't seem to clear it, ask for help from a healer, mentor, or friend. You have no other option but to move past this or stay where you are.

You know, deep down, that you're eventually going to have to face what is holding you where you are. So, why not now? Yes, it can be hard, but you have the strength and courage to do this. You have been asking for guidance for a while now, and this is your answer. Do the work, face your fears head-on, and allow yourself the freedom to move forward. Nothing is holding you back but you.

Affirmation: *I face my fears head-on and move forward with ease.*

172. COYOTE – *Trickster*

I have come to you today to let you know that someone around you is a trickster and it is affecting you.

There is a person in your life that is not being true to you. They are coming across as your best friend, saying you can confide in them, but all is not what it seems. They are breaking your trust. They carry stories to others, and they are laughing at you behind your back.

Be careful who you are putting your trust in and what you are telling them. They are going to slip up; they will say the wrong thing to someone, and it will get back to you. You will be very surprised at who it is, and you will feel very betrayed and hurt. You will get over it in time; you will find it hard to trust others for a while, but that's OK. Give yourself time to get over this, be gentle with yourself, and in time you will be able to forgive and move forward.

Affirmation: *I am gentle with myself.*

173. RACCOON – *Secrecy*

I have come to you today to say you always have an air of secrecy around you.

You have a tendency not to let your loved ones know what is going on with you; you don't tell them everything. It is not that you mistrust them, you just don't think they will understand you fully. You don't have to tell everyone everything; you just need to let them know what is going on with you on a daily basis. Maybe start by telling them the little things, then build up to the big ones.

You don't mean any harm by not telling them; you just don't think. It's become something of a habit now. Be open with everyone and see how your relationships change when you open up to what's going on and embrace the love and support they have for you, no more secrets.

Affirmation: *I embrace my openness.*

174. CHEETAH – *Procrastination*

I have come to you today to say stop procrastinating and get on with the job at hand.

You have a very bad habit of procrastinating. You leave it to the very last to take the action that you know you must. This is an old habit that you are about to let go of, once and for all. You are losing out on a lot by doing this, as you will do anything except what you should be doing. This is not good at all.

The next time you do this, be mindful of what you are doing, then stop straightaway and ask yourself why you are procrastinating. Allow yourself to go within for the answer, as this will help you clear those habits once and for all. Allow what needs to come up, and don't let the fear win. Then take the action you need to take, and it will become easier to take the action in the future.

Affirmation: *I allow myself to take the necessary action to move forward now.*

175. JAGUAR – *Gatekeeper*

I have come to you today to let you know your gatekeeper has you fully protected.

Your gatekeeper is controlling who is allowed to connect with you. They will only allow energy of the highest vibration into your energy field. Have you connected with your gatekeeper? They hold a lot of knowledge and guidance for you. You must learn to trust them, as they will help you ascend to new levels.

Build up your relationship with your gatekeeper as they will help to guide you along your path, allow new guides to connect with you, and open you up to new energies. They can also help you cleanse and clear your energy to keep in the highest vibration. You should do it on a daily basis, this will keep you and your energy clear.

Affirmation: *I am safe and protected at all times.*

176. LYNX – *Promise*

I have come to you today to say it's time to keep that promise that you have made to yourself or others.

You have made a promise to yourself or someone else, and you must keep it; there is no going back on your word. This is a commitment that you have made; you don't want to lose that trust in yourself or others. If you can't do this, then how are you going to move forward?

You are an honest, trustworthy person, so you don't want this to hold you back. If you break this promise, it's like you or the other person will lose all trust in you. They will feel they can't depend on you, and this can harm your relationship. Don't break that promise – it's not worth it, so follow through on it.

Affirmation: *I keep my promises to myself and others.*

177. OTTER – *Unite*

I have come to you today to say it's time to unite and don't let others bring you down.

You have been going through a tough time in a relationship; it's starting to affect you on all levels, and you are worried about it all the time. For you to get through this, you must unite, believe in both of you, and see the trust in your relationship.

There is part of you playing the blame game. We can all be wrong at times. You have a very strong relationship, but to get your relationship back on track, you must trust and believe in each other. Think of all the good qualities you each have and how much you love each other. Make some time for each other and get back to being united, what you do best. We all can have blips in our relationships, but the most important thing to remember is how much you love each other and how as a couple you unite.

Affirmation: *We are united in love.*

178. MOOSE – *Temporary*

I have come to you today to say this halt is temporary.

You have been very busy; you have not been looking after yourself, and you have come to a sudden stop. This is your guides saying that you must slow down. Being busy all the time and running around is not doing you any good. You don't seem to have time to do anything for yourself.

You are not receiving the guidance that you need because you are not stopping and giving yourself a minute to allow the information to come in. Spirit is asking you to stop, do your inner work, listen to the guidance you need, and then things will start moving again. They have stopped you for a reason; it's up to you to make time for yourself and allow yourself that much-needed rest before you start to move forward again.

Affirmation: *I allow myself to stop and receive.*

179. ELK – It's OK to Say No

I have come to you today to tell you it's OK to say no.

When you say no, you always feel guilty. You second-guess your decisions, and you start to worry. This has been a pattern of yours for some time now, finding it hard to say no.

Saying no does not mean that you don't care for the person; it only means you are putting up your boundaries and not letting them take advantage of your kind nature. Stop putting everyone else first and yourself last. You can't say yes to everything, and you must stop worrying about what others are saying when you don't. By saying no, you are putting your needs first, and that's a good thing, not a bad thing. Let go of the worry, put your boundaries in place, and say no. Others may be taken aback when you first say no, but that's OK – they will get used to it.

Affirmation: *It's OK to say no.*

180. HOG – *Sociable*

I have come to you today to say you are a very sociable person, and you like being out and about.

You love being out chatting, catching up with people; you are a real people person. You don't like being alone too often, as it can make you feel a bit uneasy. This can be a good thing and a bad thing. You are always the life and soul of the party; you are the one everyone counts on to turn up on a night out. Sometimes it's OK to take time out from others and give ourselves the time and space to do that much-needed inner work to allow ourselves to develop and transform.

You are too busy socialising that you are not giving yourself this time and space that is needed to go to your next level of consciousness. Clear your social calendar, switch off your phone, and do what needs to be done. Your social life will be there waiting on you. Give yourself that much-needed time to develop to your next level.

Affirmation: *I clear my social calendar to go within.*

181. LIZARD – *Messenger*

I have come to you today to say that you are missing the messages that are being sent to you.

The spirit world has been sending you messages on a daily basis, but you don't seem to be getting them. You seem to not be picking up the signs. You are doubting yourself and spirit a lot, but there is no need to. You must put your full trust and belief in spirit and the signs that you are getting; stop second-guessing the signs and messages you are receiving. You seem to just dismiss the sign and carry on as if you never got it.

It is time for you to open up and see the signs. Feel them and receive guidance. You are getting these messages because you are asking for signs and guidance, but when you do get them, you don't believe they are for you. Recognise that they are for you, allow the beautiful guidance and messages to come to you, trust and believe.

Affirmation: *I allow myself to trust and believe in the signs I receive.*

182. SCORPION – *Egypt*

I have come to you today to say you have a connection with Egypt, and it's time to honour that connection.

You are being asked to embrace your connection with Egypt; this can bring you onto a different path. You had a past life in Egypt, and you have an Egyptian guide. This is your time to connect into this lifetime and see who you were. When you connect in with past lives, you can clear what needs to be cleared, release vows, contracts, and bindings that hold us in this lifetime. It can also help us to remember and reawaken our knowledge and gifts from this lifetime.

Go ahead and connect in with this lifetime, see all you need, clear what needs to be cleared, reawaken your gifts, and unleash your knowledge. There is so much waiting for you.

Affirmation: *I unleash my hidden knowledge and gifts now.*

183. GOLDFISH – *Bowl*

I have come to you today to say you feel like you are in a goldfish bowl, going around and around and getting nowhere.

You have got yourself into a state, and you can't seem to get yourself out again. You feel trapped. Look at these feelings, go deep within and see what the cause is behind those feelings. Are you causing these feelings, or is someone else? If it's somebody else, then step out of their energy, clear, ground, cut the cords that are holding you to this person, and let it go.

If it's yours, then see what or who is causing you to feel like this. Journal on how it is making you feel, then ground, cut, and clear your energy. Let it go as it does not serve you as you move forward.

Affirmation: *I give myself permission to be free.*

184. WOMBAT – *Aggressive*

I have come to you today to say you or someone around you is being very aggressive in the way they are doing things.

If it is you, go within, feel and see what is causing this, as it is not normal for you to feel and act this way. You may be feeling a bit out of sorts – this is the way it is presented to you. Allow yourself to go deep and relax. This energy you're holding onto is causing this aggression and you have to let it go, as it is doing you no good. As you do the inner work, you will start to feel this aggression ease up; you will feel so much better and be back to yourself soon.

If it is somebody else, make them aware of how they are acting, and how it's making you feel. Ask them to go deep within, and if they can't do it alone, ask them to get help as they need to deal with what is going on for them. They may not be aware that they are affecting you with their behaviour.

Affirmation: *I release all the anger I hold within with love.*

185. CHIPMUNK – *Adventurers*

I have come to you today to say you feel like going on a bit of adventure; this is so not like you.

Go ahead, be adventurous! Go grab life with both hands. When you feel like this, there is no stopping you; you feel a huge sense of freedom. You like it when you feel like this, as you're able to make choices and decisions with ease, which normally you find hard.

To keep yourself in this vibration, pay attention to how you are feeling when you are like this; feel it, see it, and keep your energy clear. Then you should be able to keep yourself in this vibration. No matter what goes on around you, you can stay in this vibration if you believe it and feel it. Allow yourself to grab life with both hands.

Affirmation: *I allow myself to grab life with both hands.*

186. POSSUM – *Underestimated*

I have come to you today to say you are underestimating your gifts.

With your gifts, you have the ability to help others on their souls' journey. You don't seem to realise how special you are and how your gifts can help others. You are seriously undermining yourself. You have allowed other people to project their opinions on you, and your own self-doubt plays a part as well. The only people you should be listening to are yourself and your guides, as they have your best interests at heart. Push aside the ego of others as well as your own ego and self-doubt, and allow yourself to see and stand in your own power.

You have come here to Earth at this time to help others free their souls and to help them see how amazing they are. You can't help others if you don't see, believe, and trust your own gifts. It's time to let it all go and step onto your path fully and fulfil your soul's contract.

Affirmation: *I see, believe, and trust my soul's mission now.*

187. HYENA – *Community*

I have come here today to say it's time to get yourself out into the community.

There is a need for you to go out and join a group or organise one. This is something that's been on your mind for a while. When you join the community, you will become aware of how alone you have been feeling. You will start to feel like you belong to something now. This is going to bring you a whole new lease of life.

You will start to feel happy and secure; this will have a major effect on your life, and you will notice the difference straight away. You will gain new friends and a whole new way of looking at life. Go ahead, there is nothing stopping you from joining the group; this will liberate you and bring in that sense of belonging that you so much want. There is no time like the present.

Affirmation: *I allow myself to be a part of the community now.*

188. CHIMPANZEE – *Understanding Oneself*

I have come to you today to say it is time for you to understand yourself.

This is a time to go within and really look at what makes you tick. What are your core values? What dreams do you want to achieve? What do you judge and what triggers you? What emotions are you carrying and why are you holding on to them? Why do certain people trigger you? Why do you do the things you do? What decisions do you want to make? What dreams do you want to fulfil?

When you have all the answers, you get a better understanding of yourself, then you can let go of what needs to go. Concentrate on what you want to bring in and take the necessary actions. Understanding ourselves is one of the most important things we can do.

Affirmation: *I allow myself to understand myself.*

189. JELLYFISH – *The Power of Intention*

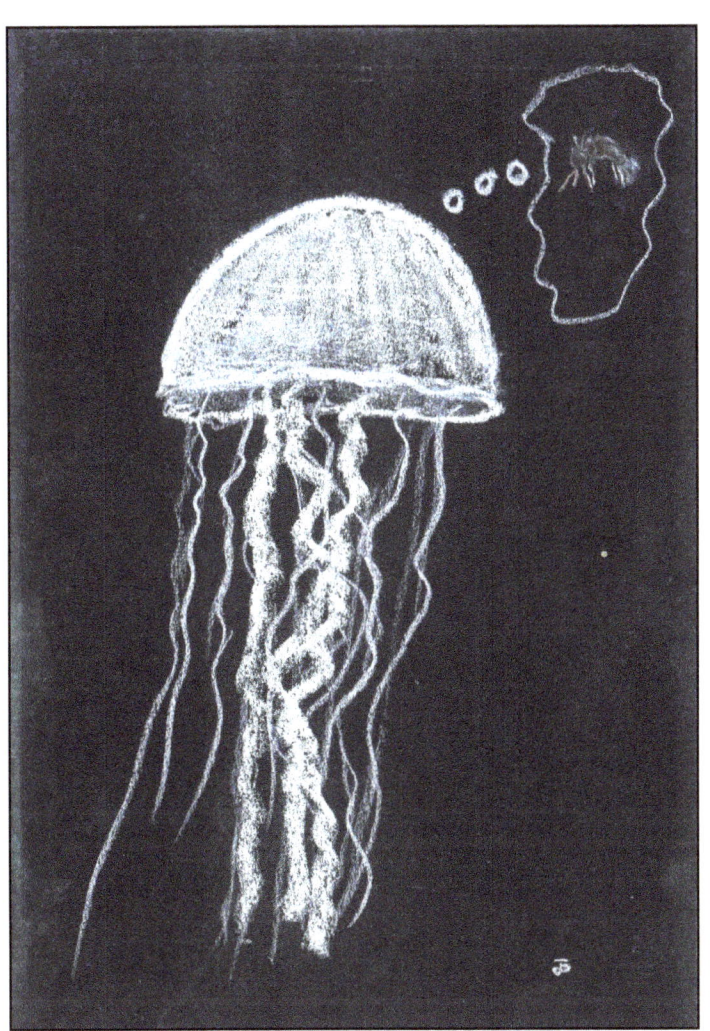

I have come to you today to say it's time you put the power of intention to work.

It's time for you to truly work with the universe and allow them to show you how the power of intention works. This can be very powerful, so be careful of your thoughts – you must keep them positive. The power of intention works in three steps: decide what you want, get clear on your why (this is very important), and visualise it.

Do your visualisation every day, and believe and trust that the universe will bring it to you. Don't get caught up in the 'how' – just allow. Set the intention and it will come to you. Start on something small, and then set your intentions bigger. Remember it can come to you in any form, so just allow and open yourself up to all possibilities. Be positive, use your intention, believe, and trust.

Affirmation: *Energy goes where attention flows.*

190. SQUIRREL – Last Minute

I have come to you today to tell you to stop leaving everything to the last minute.

You have a tendency to leave everything to the last minute, but this is not serving you at all. You just put it all off until you have to do it, and this is putting you under a lot of unnecessary pressure, causing you to go into overwhelm, feeling stressed, and then you don't want to do it at all.

Why not start getting things done when you first know they need to be done? Just do them straightaway where possible, so you are not leaving it all to accumulate. Do one thing at a time; you will see the difference when you do this, as you will get so much more done. You won't go into stress, and you will find it easy to keep on top of things. You will be much more organised; you will feel so much better within yourself, and you might even enjoy doing it.

Affirmation: *I am motivated and organised.*

191. BAT – *Misunderstood*

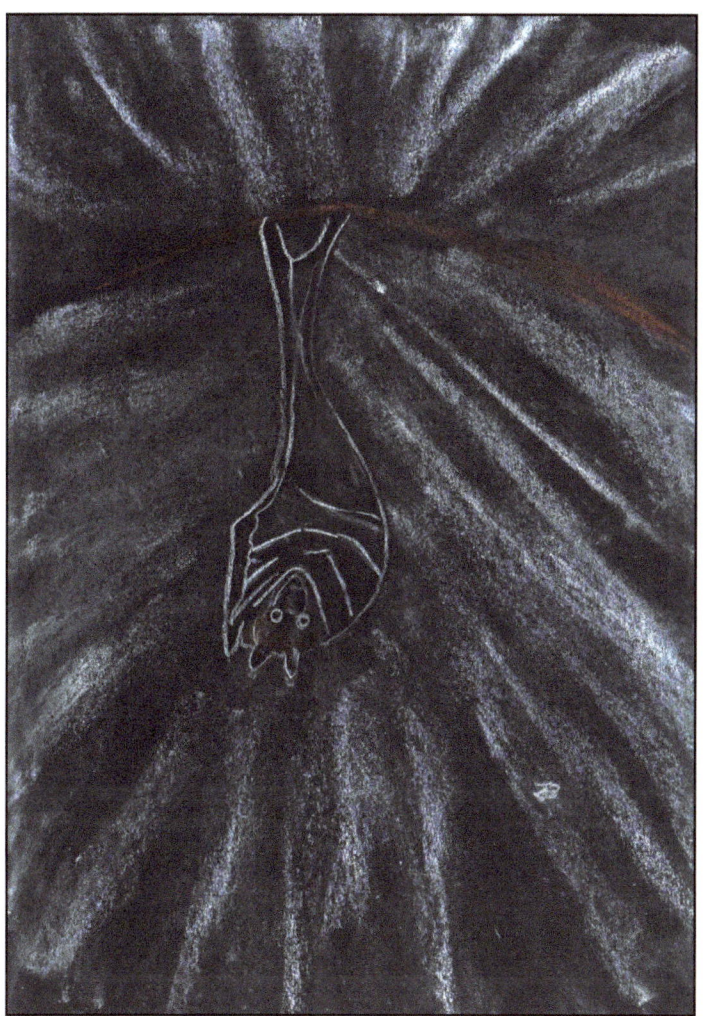

I have come to you today to say you are being misunderstood by many.

It is the way you come across to some people – sometimes, they don't know what way to take you. You can give off the wrong energy vibe at times, and this can be taken the wrong way. You can feel this from some people when you are around them, and you get that feeling that nobody understands you. You have a deep feeling of being alone.

The key to this is to communicate clearly and tell others what you want or don't want. Don't get caught up in what others think of you – that is none of your business, so step out of the energy of that. Be open to other opinions but hold onto your own and be yourself. Not everyone will understand you, and that's OK. Understand yourself and be true to you.

Affirmation: *I am my own unique person.*

192. HARE – *Ancestral Healing*

I have come to you today to say it's time to heal your ancestral line.

This is a very important part of your transformation. This is a way of freeing yourself from feelings of low self-worth, unhealthy patterns, limiting beliefs around money, sickness, illness, self-sabotage, and family trauma.

We hold onto these in our cellular memories, and this can hold us back on so many levels. When we choose to heal our ancestral line, we do this for all our family, and the next generation can be free from these patterns.

Call on me and your guides to see what you are holding onto and ask for this to be healed. If you feel you can't do this alone, get some help from a healer or shaman to help you go deep and heal your ancestral line. This is not an easy thing to do, but you have the strength to do it. This will bring you the transformation you have been looking for. Also, it will set you free and your children, your children's children, and so on.

Affirmation: *I heal my ancestral line with love.*

193. FROG – *Education*

I have come to you today to tell you it's time to go back to study.

There is a certain program that you have been thinking about for a while now. You have been saying, 'I will do it when I have time or when the time is right.' This is the time for you to stop putting it off and go for it – no more stopping yourself. This will open you up to a whole new way of looking at yourself and your life.

You will learn so much about yourself on this journey. This will allow your soul to open and expand to the next level. You have the ability to do this, so stop doubting yourself, and allow yourself to step forward into the new. Yes, it can be hard at times to start something new, but this is your time. Allow your soul to expand to the next level through study and unlocking your inner wisdom.

Affirmation: *I unlock my soul's wisdom.*

194. MOLE – *True/False*

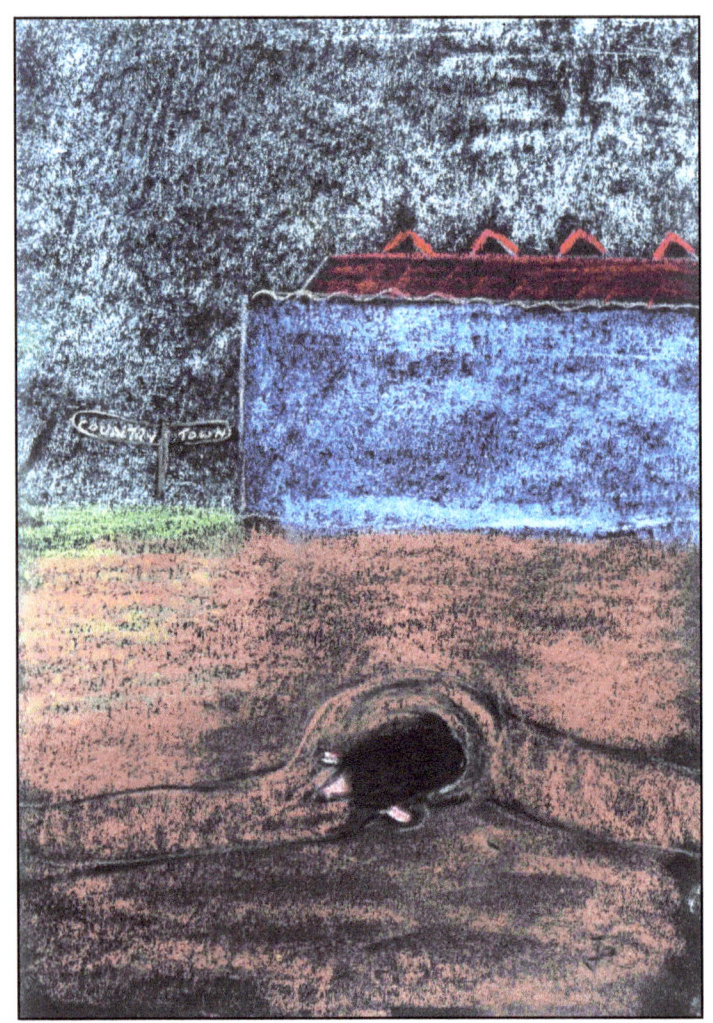

I have come to you today to say you have a very strong knowing when it comes to what is true and what is false. You can read a situation to a T, but you don't always trust this ability. Now is the time to really develop this knowing of yours. It can serve you very well in life. You must learn to trust this more, and don't let others string you along. When it happens, you always say, 'I should have listened to myself.'

Trust in this feeling – it will never let you down. You have learned so many hard lessons when you didn't trust it, but when you trusted your knowing, it worked out very differently. Believe and trust in your knowing, and you will see your life go in a different direction.

Affirmation: *I trust my knowing.*

195. ANT – *Effort*

I have come to you today to say it's time to put the effort in and stop doing things by halves.

You want to have a great career, new job, nice home, and a new car, but what are you doing to bring this into your life? We all want the finer things in life, but you have to make the effort to go get them, as they will not come by themselves. You just seem to be plodding through life. You say you are not happy with the way life is going, but you are not doing anything to change it, and nobody else can do it for you.

You must set a goal and go for it. Ask yourself what you want, what you truly want, then make a plan and take action. It's up to you to keep taking the action; as you take the action, your life will start to change for the better. This will inspire you to keep moving forward. You have the strength and courage to have it all and more – you just have to go get it.

Affirmation: *I commit to myself 100%.*

196. BEETLE – *Insignificant*

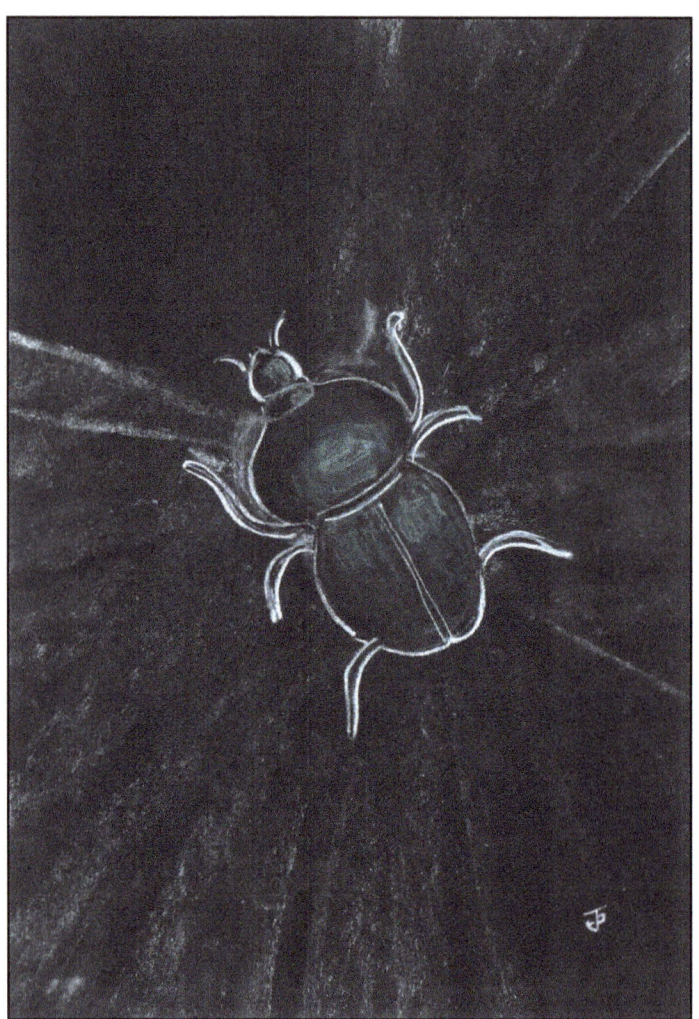

I have come to you today to say you are feeling insignificant in life. Are you feeling that you are not worthy?

I am here to help you see what you truly are and that it is OK to feel this way at times. The most important part is that you recognise it, and now you can do the inner work to make yourself feel worthy of everything.

You have amazing gifts that the world needs – and yes, you are worthy of sharing them. Look within and see the beauty of your soul, full of light. This is the light that the world sees. You may not see this light at the moment, so go deep within and let go of the insignificant feelings you may have. Unlock and see your true self; allow your light to shine and shine bright.

Affirmation: *I am worthy of my dreams.*

197. DRAGONFLY – *Deep Thought*

I have come to you today to say let go of your deep thoughts.

You can go into your thoughts on a very deep level at times, and this can knock you out of balance and into worry. You can get stuck on a thought, and it eats away at you, and then you get yourself into a pickle.

This is a habit of yours at the moment; you do notice it at times and pull yourself back, but each time you go into worry, you are finding it harder and longer to come back into balance. You have recognised the habit, so now is the time to change it – only you can do this. Every time you feel yourself going into worry, counteract it with a positive thought. The more you do this, the more positivity you will attract into your life and the less worry you will have; this will bring in big changes. Embrace the change and let go of the deep thoughts.

Affirmation: *I have the power to create change now.*

198. HUMMINGBIRD – *Little Pleasures*

I have come to you today to say look at all the little pleasures you have, and don't always be looking for the big expensive things. You can get so much more out of the little things in life.

When you see and appreciate the little things, you come from a place of gratitude, and when you come from a place of gratitude, everything is possible. You start attracting little pleasures into your life. Sometimes we just need to be shown how wonderful the little pleasures are so we can appreciate them and be grateful for all we have.

Look around you at this moment in time, see all the beautiful things you have, and be grateful. Do this on a regular basis; you will notice the more you are grateful for the little pleasures, you will attract more, and you will see the world from a different place.

Affirmation: *I appreciate life's little pleasures.*

199. TORTOISE – *Harmony*

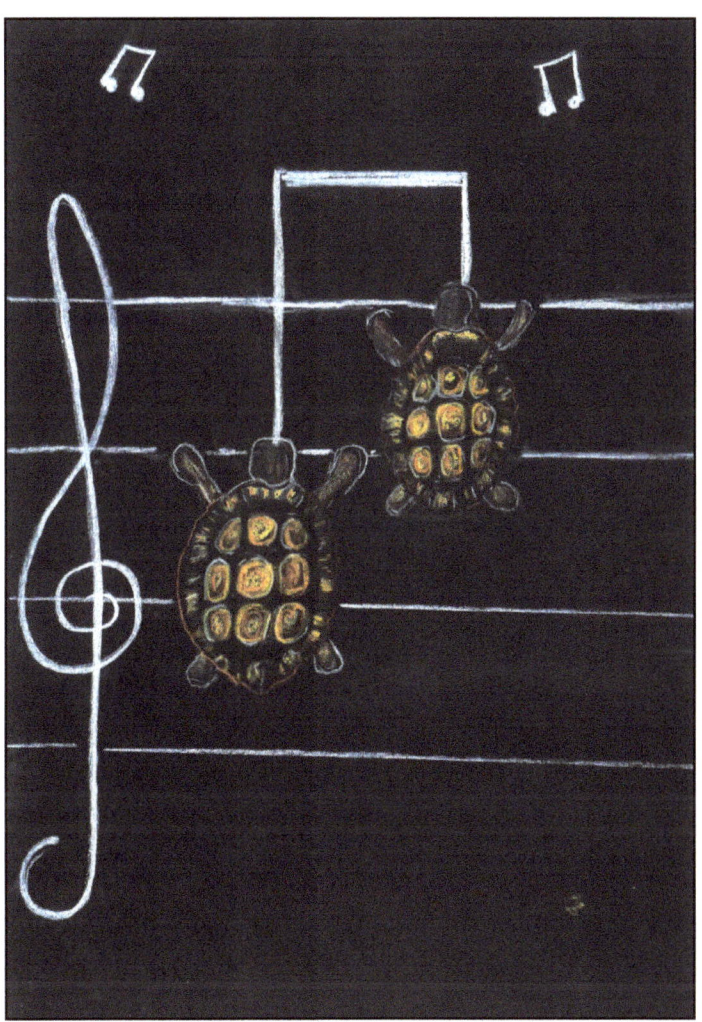

I have come to you today to say it's time to bring peace and harmony into your life.

You have been struggling for some time now, trying to get peace and harmony into your life. You just can't seem to get there; this is the one thing you want most in your life. For you to bring this into your life, you must look at all areas that are causing you to struggle. Don't just look at them on the surface, you must dig deep within and ask yourself what needs to change. Be truthful with yourself; ask the question, 'How are you going to change?'

The answers are there, but are you willing to go within and get them? That is up to you now, as no one can do this for you. Are you brave enough? How bad do you want peace and harmony? Peace and harmony are waiting, but only you can bring this into your life.

Affirmation: *I am willing to go deep within to bring peace and harmony into my life now.*

200. SNAIL – *What is Your Hurry?*

I have come to you today to say, what is your hurry?

Rome was not built in a day. Nor will your spirituality. You are always pushing and want it all now, but you must go through certain things in life before you reach your destination. It is the same with your spiritual journey.

You must learn to enjoy the journey. Enjoy every moment in time, not always rushing to the next thing, as this will only wear you out, and you will go into burnout mode. Spirit has a way of stopping us in our tracks if we don't listen and slow down.

Sometimes the best thing you can do for yourself on your spiritual journey is to pause, take it all in, acknowledge all you have achieved to date, rest and get ready for the next leg of your journey. This is what you must do at this moment in time. Yes, stop, rest, and replenish. Remember it is not the destination that counts – it's the journey along your spiritual path.

Affirmation: *I gave myself permission to stop, rest, and replenish for the next leg of my journey.*

201. BLACK SWAN – *Making the Impossible Possible*

I have come to you today to say you have the ability to make the impossible possible. You have great strength and courage; you can have the impossible if you really want to. You have always found ways to get what another feels is impossible to get. This is a gift of yours.

You have never really looked at it like this before, as it comes so naturally to you. It's like a switch that turns on in you, and you go for it. You focus on the job at hand, and you never lose sight of it. So many have asked you to explain this, but you cannot – it's just you. Don't stop what you are doing; go ahead, make the impossible possible, and just allow yourself to be you.

Affirmation: *Everything is possible with belief.*

202. WOODPECKER – *Never One to Give Up*

I have come to you today to say you are never one to give up on anything in life, so why start now?

You always keep going, no matter what, and you never give up – so why are you giving up now? Yes, life can get hard, and it can be difficult. You have been through so much, and now you feel you just can't seem to keep going.

Yes, you have the strength to keep going; you just need to rest yourself, maybe take a bit of time out before you start again. You can do this, you just need to rest; you have all you need within you to get through this, so don't stop now just before the finish line.

Affirmation: *I have the strength and courage to keep going.*

203. SALMON – *Living Life to the Fullest*

I have come to you today to say it is time to start living your life to the fullest.

Yes, start living life to the fullest; what is stopping you? You only get one life, so live it. Stop saying, 'What if this, what if that?' It might never happen. You are only on this planet for a short while, so live your life, and have no regrets.

You can get so caught up in what might happen that you miss out on the moment. You get so caught in fear and worry that life is passing you by, and you are not living the best possible life. Grip life with both hands, go and live your life to the fullest, let go of 'what if', fear and worry – life is too short. Live in the moment.

Affirmation: *I allow myself to live life in the moment.*

204. DOG – *Selfless*

I have come to you today to say you are such a selfless person who puts everyone else's needs before your own.

This can be a good thing and a bad thing as you can give too much of yourself to others at your own detriment, and when this happens, you get out of balance or sometimes sick. You wonder why this happens.

You must keep yourself balanced as you need your energy for yourself; you can help others, but you are not to forget about yourself and your needs. You feel selfish at times when you put yourself first, but that is not the case. It is important that you look after yourself first, then you can help others, then it's a win-win for everyone, and you are in perfect balance.

Affirmation: *I give myself permission to take time for me.*

205. CAT – *Quirky*

I have come to you today to say get your quirky side out and stop hiding it.

You have a very quirky side that you hide from everyone, but not anymore. Now is your time to shine and allow the world to see the real you. You have so much to offer the world, and you are hiding this side of you.

You have tried to fit in, and this made you feel miserable, sad, and lonely. You don't need to try and fit in anymore, you are who you are. Stop and look in the mirror and appreciate yourself, quirkiness and all.

The only thing that will make you truly happy is to be yourself and be proud of who you are; if we were all the same, the world would be a very dull place. Step out and take centre stage of your life now.

Affirmation: *It is safe for me to be myself now.*

206. HORSE – *Appetite for Life*

I have come to you today to ask, have you lost your appetite for life?

You seem to have lost that 'get up and go', the drive that you had for life. You have let life get in your way and can't seem to get that drive back.

Yes, you can do it, you have that determination within you to do anything, but you just can't seem to see to access it at the moment. That's OK, it happens.

Drop into your heart and ask yourself what you will do to get it back; you hold the answer within you.

When you get the answer, make a plan, take action, and you will see how easy it is to get that appetite for life back.

Affirmation: *I have limitless drive and willpower.*

207. MOUSE – *What You Missed?*

I have come to you today to ask, what have you missed?

There is an important aspect of your life that you seem to be overlooking to move forward.

You want to move forward so much that you seem to be focusing on the direction, but you have missed something, and that something is a vital piece of the puzzle. I am asking you to step back and look at all the pieces of the puzzle individually, then sit and ask yourself what you have missed.

It will take you a while to see it, but that's OK. For now, you must breathe and open yourself up to all possibilities.

Pushing gets you nowhere. Allow with ease, and it will all fall into place.

Affirmation: *I allow it all to flow with ease and grace.*

208. RABBIT – *Spontaneity*

I have come to you today to ask, have you lost your spontaneity in life?

You have lost the spontaneous side of yourself, and you seem to be letting life get you down. You are overthinking every decision that you are making, and sometimes you can't seem to be able to make any at all, which is not good.

Now is the time to change and let your spontaneous side out again. The next time you feel yourself going into indecision, step back and ask yourself what is really going on at that moment in time. Ask yourself, is this really you? Do you really want to do this? If so, just go for it.

It will take a while for you to break the old habit but being aware is half the battle. No more holding yourself back, allow the spontaneous side of yourself out to play now.

Affirmation: *I allow my spontaneous side out now.*

209. SPIDER – *Entangled*

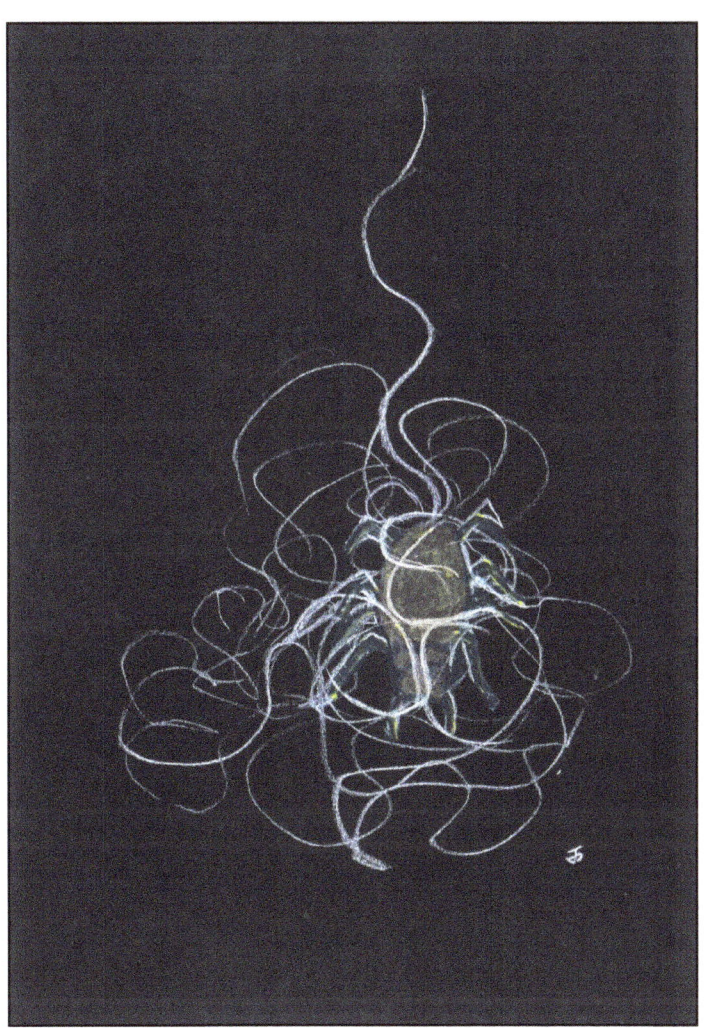

I have come to you today to say you have yourself entangled in so much at this moment in time, and you can't seem to get yourself out of it.

You have so much going on at the moment, and your attention is being drawn to everything. You are so entangled in all the details of everything and everyone that you can't seem to see what is truly going on. Now is the time to stop, stop, stop, then you must ground yourself.

Take a look at what you are doing to yourself, ask yourself why you are so entangled in everything and not looking at the real situation at hand. You feel if you keep yourself entangled, you won't have to face the truth, and it might go away. But, it won't – you must untangle and deal with what you have been putting off for some time now. You can do this; yes, it might be hard at first, but it will be worth it in the end. Go within and face what needs to be faced. You have the strength and courage to overcome this.

Affirmation: *I allow myself to see my real self.*

210. FOX – *Swift*

I have come to you today to say you can be a very swift thinker when you are in a jam.

This is one of your gifts, and a great gift to have. Sometimes you second-guess this, but you must trust this at all times.

There is a situation coming up in the next few weeks or months that will require you to put that swift thinking into action. You have the ability to overcome this, but you must trust yourself 100% and not listen to outside influences. You will know what to do straight away, so don't let others talk you into doing it their way, as you know what is right for you. You know deep down it will work out for you; you must take the action that you know in your heart is right for you. Don't let others change your mind; keep true to yourself and take swift action. All will be well.

Affirmation: *I listen and trust myself 100%.*

211. STAG – *Regeneration*

I have come to you today to say you are going through a spiritual regeneration at the moment.

You have been through a tough time, or you still are going through it. You are going through this because this is a lesson that you have come here to learn, and you will continue to go through this time and time again until you have learnt the lesson. This is part of your soul journey.

You will be letting go of old habits and patterns, and even some old emotions as you go through this. You are a strong person, and you will get through this; be gentle with yourself and remember you can always ask for help if you are finding it too hard. Sometimes we need help to clear the deep stuff.

Just remember this too shall pass. When it does, you will step into your next level of consciousness and move forward along your spiritual path. Keep yourself grounded at all times. You can come out the other end.

Affirmation: *This too shall pass.*

212. WOLF – *Lack of Trust*

I have come to you today to say you have a lack of trust in people around you at the moment.

You can't seem to trust anyone around you for no good reason. Are you sure it's not your own trust issues? You don't trust anyone, and you question everything others say and do to you. This is starting to really affect your life, and it's causing a lot of concern for you.

There is a deep issue going on here for you. I do feel that you just can't trust yourself, and you are projecting this onto others. You must go within on a deep level to get to the bottom of this, or you will drive yourself mad questioning everyone and everything.

Get the help of a healer, mentor, or shaman to help you overcome this. This is a past issue that you have buried deep within, and now is the time to face it head-on and release it, so it no longer has any control over you. You can do this.

Affirmation: *I choose trust over doubt.*

213. CROW – *Walk Your Talk*

I have come to you today to ask, are you ready to walk your talk?

If so, why aren't you doing it? You are great at giving others advice on what they should and should not be doing, but you don't seem to listen to it for yourself. Now is your time to step out and go for it. There is nothing holding you back except yourself.

All the advice you have given to others, now is your time to take it on board for yourself. What would you say to others if they were you? Give yourself that advice and get to it. Make yourself a plan and stick to it, one step at a time, so you don't get overwhelmed. Take the leap of faith; it's much easier to do than to not do it. There is no time like the present to make the first move; yes, you can do it. The first step is always the hardest, but go ahead and step forward now.

Affirmation: *I am ready to walk my talk now.*

214. BULL – *Stand Your Ground*

I have come to you today to say stand your ground and dig your heels in.

You know that you are right in this instance and that you are not going to back down. You know that you did nothing wrong, and what is going on is not your fault, but others seem to think differently.

You know the real reason others are trying to point the finger of blame at you; they can't seem to listen to the truth, but that's their problem, not yours. When they are ready, they will listen and hear the truth. But until then, they will blame you. It will all come out in the end.

You must stand your ground and dig your heels in deep; do not budge, no matter how hard it gets. Even if it means an easier life, do not give in this time – you always do, and they know that, but not this time. It will sort itself out in a while, but until then, I suggest you practice forgiveness. You can get through this, and all will be well again.

Affirmation: *Stand your ground, no matter what.*

215. RAM – *Defiant Attitude*

I have come to you today to say it's time to show that defiant attitude you have within you to the world.

You have a side of you that you don't like a lot of people to see, as it can bring out the worst in you. You have a very defiant attitude towards some things, and you try to hide it. You don't seem to like this side of yourself, but now is the time for you to accept this part of you, as it can come useful as you go through life. Look at this attitude you have as a gift, not a hindrance, and this will change the whole way you will look at things. Acceptance is key to the way we live our lives; self-acceptance is very important. Show this side of you and be proud of who you are.

Affirmation: *I accept myself just the way I am.*

216. BADGER – *Inner Voice*

I have come to you today to ask, can you hear your inner voice? It's calling you!

You hear this voice within your head at times, and you think you are going mad; well, you are not. This is your inner voice, your knowing, your soul, your spirit, or whatever you want to call it.

It is trying to lead you down a different path, but you don't seem to be hearing this, or you are dismissing it. It won't go away as you have awakened your inner voice. You may be only starting on your path, or you are evolving to your next level of consciousness. They are trying to give you messages to help you move forward with ease and flow. The next time you get the feeling/sign, trust and take the action, and see how life will just flow. You will learn to trust and believe.

Affirmation: *I trust and believe in myself.*

217. ROBIN – *Decluttering*

I have come to you today to say, it's time to declutter your space.

What are you holding on to that is blocking your way forward? This may be on a spiritual level or a physical level.

If it is on a spiritual level, you must go deep within and see what it is that is blocking you from moving forward. You may need the help of a mentor, healer, shaman etc…

On physical level, take a good look around and see what you are hoarding and what needs to go. Make three piles: Bin, Donate, Sentimental. Leave the sentimental one until last. When you have this done, do a cleaning ritual on your space and clear all unwanted energies.

By doing this you will be able to move forward to new things as you have made space for the new to come in.

Affirmation: *I release to move forward.*

218. EAGLE – Hope

I have come to you today to say hold on to hope and never let it go.

You must hold on to the hope that you have. We need the energy of hope with us, so when things are not going to plan, we have something to hold on to.

No matter what is going on, if we have hope, we can get through anything, and this is one of those times. Life is about to throw you a curveball, but you have the strength and hope, and you will get through this. You have gotten through much worse than this, so hold on, call on your inner strength, see the hope, and allow it to unfold the way it's meant to. You will get through this, as you always do. It may look much worse than it is but sit back, bring the energy of hope in and see how your view will change – and then it will all change. Never give up on hope.

Affirmation: *I have hope, and I am hope.*

219. BLACKBIRD – *Culture*

I have come to you today to say it is time for you to learn more about your family lineage.

There is a pattern that you have going on in your life at the moment that you can't seem to kick. You have to look at the triggers to help you kick this. Now is the time to look at your ancestral/cultural lineage, as that is where the patterns are. When you do this, you will then have to do the healing/clearing on this to clear the timelines; you will be clearing for you and your children, and your children's children. You will be able to see how and why these patterns are affecting you; when you do this type of healing, you do it for your family as well.

As you do this deep work, you will see the pattern unfold, and you will be setting yourself free. Be gentle with yourself as you go through this, and remember to ask for help if you need it.

Affirmation: *I heal and move forward with love.*

220. WEASEL – *Self-Judgement*

I have come to you today to say stop the self-judgement, NOW!

You have gotten into a bad habit of judging yourself, but there is no need to be doing this. You have been looking at all the things you think you are doing wrong. Well, you're not doing anything wrong. You are who you are, so stop.

When we judge ourselves, we put more blocks in our way. We get so caught up in all we are doing wrong and can't seem to see how amazing we are. Look at how far you have come and all you have achieved to date. Set the negativity aside and look at the positive. When you catch yourself judging yourself, stop and say, 'Cancel, clear and delete.' Follow it with a positive thought; you will soon see your thoughts change, and you will start to see how amazing you are. Now is your time to look at what you want to bring in for the future and go for it.

Affirmation: *I see how amazing I am.*

221. BUFFALO – *Brave Face*

I have come to you today to say stop putting on a brave face.

Why do you always put on a brave face to others? Why can't you just let them see how you are feeling? This is a habit of yours; you don't want anyone to see how you are truly feeling.

You have so much going on inside that you are like a bomb waiting to explode; this is not good at all. You have been holding on for years, and you just can't seem to let it go. Now is the time to let all this go; write or just say how you are feeling, get some healing done, and allow all that is held within you out. Your throat chakra and solar plexus need the most work. You will find as you start healing, you will be able to talk and let others know how you feel. You will be surprised how many people are there to help you let all this pent-up emotion out. No more putting on a brave face; you are who you are, so embrace yourself.

Affirmation: *I allow myself to express my true feelings now.*

222. ELEPHANT – *Commitment*

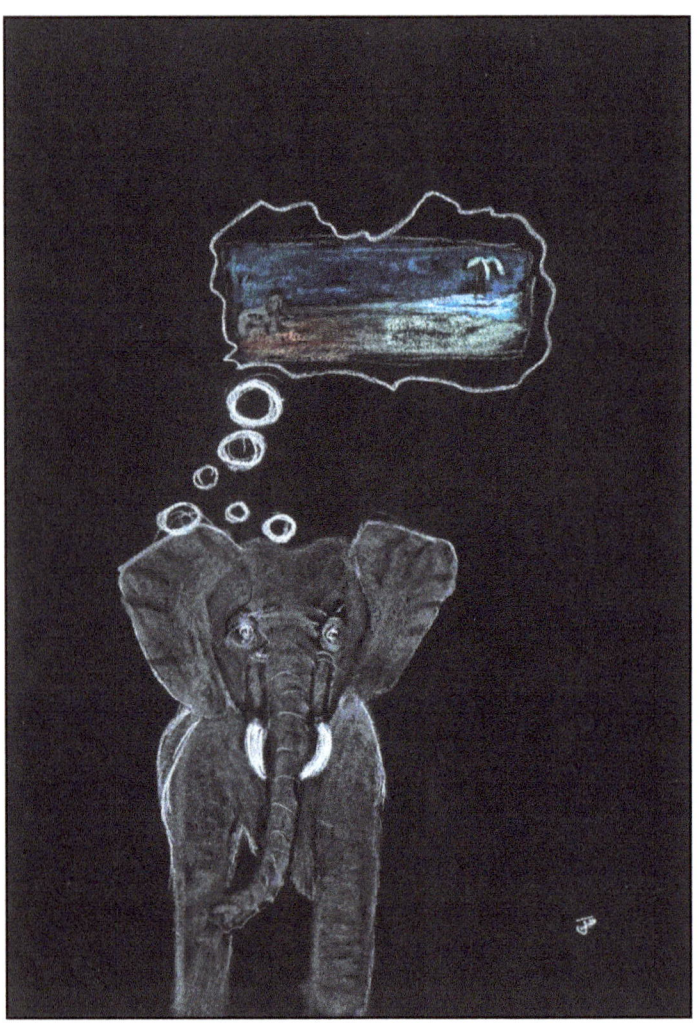

I have come to you today to ask, are you truly committed to your dreams?

Are you fully committed, or are you allowing all the opportunities to pass you by? Yes, we can say we are committed, but then we don't do the action – we just allow it to pass us by. I feel you are doing this at this moment in time.

You are not sure what you really want, and this is what is stopping you from moving forward. Sit down, ask yourself what your heart truly desires, and then make a plan of action. When you know what you truly want, you will be 100% committed.

Dreams do come true; dream it, feel it, and be committed, and then it will all fall into place.

Affirmation: *I am 100% committed to my dreams.*

223. LIONESS – Command

I have come to you today to say it's time for you to have a chat with your guides and command the change you want.

You have been looking to change things in your life for some time now, but you just can't seem to get there. Every time you take a step forward, you seem to be pulled right back. You are starting to ask yourself if you are on the right path, or what is truly going on. Now is the time to sit and command the answer to these questions; be open to receiving the answers, no matter what. Sometimes we ask, but we are not open to receiving the answer, or we don't like the answer we receive. Have you learnt the lesson? Are you holding on to something that is not serving you? When we command the answers from our guides, we will get the answers. Be open and trust what you receive.

Affirmation: *I move forward with ease and flow.*

224. WHITE TIGER – *War*

I have come to you today to say you seem to be at war with yourself.

You have an inner battle going on at the moment, and it is causing you to question everything that you know. There are two aspects of yourself that are very different – one side of you sees everything spiritual, and the other side sees 3D.

You must look at the side that is causing you the conflict at the moment (3D). Ask it why and what it is here to show you; start a dialogue with it – you will be surprised at what it will bring up for you. This is coming up now for you to go to your next level of consciousness. You must do the healing on this, but if you can't do it alone, get the help that you need. You can't go forward without this healing taking place. Don't worry, you will get through this; it's just another level, a different devil. It's your time to heal, and as you do this, you will come back into balance and inner peace.

Affirmation: *I listen to my inner voice.*

225. WHALE – *Watch Your Words*

I have come to you today to say, watch your words, as you are a great manifester, and you don't want to manifest what you don't want.

You must be very careful of what you are saying. You have been wondering how you are getting everything you don't want, and you just can't seem to see how it happens. It's what you are saying that is causing this, so be careful as you will attract what you don't want. Be very precise with your words and always be positive, and when you do this, you will see that you start attracting all the good things in life. Always show gratitude, no matter how small it is. If you say something negative, always say, 'Cancel, clear and delete' straight after it. Your word is your wand, so go ahead and manifest what you want.

Affirmation: *I am a powerful manifestor.*

226. LADYBIRD – *Invest*

I have come to you today to say it's time you invested in yourself.

You have been thinking about this for some time now. You keep saying, 'When I have the money, I will,' but you don't seem to get there.

Well, now is that time to invest in yourself – yes, now! Don't worry about where you will get the money from. Ask if you can do a payment plan; you will never know if you don't ask. Also, ask your guides to bring you the money you need – trust, and you will receive.

Once you have made the decision to do this course/mentorship program, you have opened yourself up to receive the money for it. It is all about the decision – the rest falls into place. Don't forget to hand it over to the universe and open yourself up to receive.

Affirmation: *When I invest in myself, everyone wins.*

227. HAMSTER – *Enjoy Your Achievements*

I have come to you today to say you deserve to enjoy your achievements.

You have worked so hard to get where you are today, but you can't seem to enjoy it. You are looking at what comes next, where you need to go, and what more needs to be done. It is like you don't feel you deserve it. You must stop and look around you and see what you have achieved. Yes, your dream has come true. Now is the time for you to pause and celebrate your achievements; it is not every day your dreams come true.

Enjoy this moment in time as this is what you have worked so hard for. Don't be worried about what comes next. Relax and take time out. Your next venture will come when you are ready, but for now, enjoy all your achievements, and the rest will unfold.

Affirmation: *I truly deserve what I have achieved.*

228. RAT – *Shrewd*

I have come to you today to say you must be very shrewd at the moment.

You watch what others are doing and how they act, and you can see if they are sincere or not. You can see right through people. You see the way others can manipulate those around them. You need to be on your guard as they will try and do it to you. This is where your shrewdness comes in; they can try, but you can read them like a book so you will not fall into their trap.

You know deep down when they are trying to do this, and it is an amazing gift, as you don't let others take advantage of you. You are very sharp, you pay attention, you listen, and you take it all in before you act on it – this will serve you well. You must be very clear in the way you deal with others. Don't battle fire with fire. Look and listen before you act.

Affirmation: *I look and listen before I act.*

229. PIG – *Mysteries*

I have come to you today to say, there seems to be an air of mystery around you at the moment.

You seem to be keeping everything close to your chest, and you don't want anyone to know what is going on. This can be both a good thing and a bad thing. You have lost your trust in people, and you are finding it hard to confide in others. Your trust has been broken before, and you are afraid to trust again in case it happens again. You feel safer by not letting others know what is going on for you.

Yes, I can understand this, but not everyone is like that; you are going to have to put your trust in someone someday, so start with something small and then you can take it from there. You must learn to trust yourself first, then others.

Affirmation: *It is OK to trust myself and others.*

230. HEN – *Sharp*

I have come to you today to say your awareness is very sharp at the moment.

You seem to be able to pick up on everything at the moment, and you seem to be able to see what is right for you and what isn't.

You have a great sense of awareness that is very sharp. When people are not being true to you or have a different agenda going on in the background, you get that knowing feeling, and you know deep down that all is not what it seems.

It is like your awareness is on high alert and it is not allowing you to take on other people's stuff. You must trust this at all times, as it will never let you down and it will keep you from making mistakes or going in the wrong direction. Always trust your gut reaction – never question it as it will never steer you wrong.

Affirmation: *I trust and believe in my knowing.*

231. PEACOCK – *Beauty*

I have come to you today to ask if you can see your beauty within.

You seem to think you are not good enough or worthy enough for your dreams to come true. You are only seeing what is wrong in your life or the negative things about yourself. You don't see what others see, your beauty, your light, your kindness. How you help others and what love you give to everyone around you. You are a beautiful soul who has so much to give to the world – you just can't see it.

It is time now to take a long hard look at yourself, see past the fog of illusion you have around you, and see your true beauty, the beauty everyone else sees. Your light is so bright; you must allow it to shine and shine bright. The world needs your light, and there are many people waiting for you and your light, so allow your true beautiful self to shine bright.

Affirmation: *I see past the illusions; I see my true, beautiful self now.*

232. DOLPHIN – *Resurrection*

I have come to you today to say you are going through a tough time, but you will soon resurrect your true divine self.

You have been going around and around, and you have asked for help from your spiritual team; they have heard your cry for help. It is like no matter what you try, you can't seem to get yourself out of it, and you are losing your faith a little.

Now more than ever, you must hold on to your faith as it is all about to change, and your prayers are being answered. You will rise from this, so hold on tight, as we are getting the last few things into place before this resurrection can happen.

You will be like the dolphin and rise above the water to inhale the air you need to overcome this. So, hold on, as things are about to change, but not the way you might think. Be open and receive.

Affirmation: *I hold onto my faith as change is upon me now.*

233. WHALE – *Importance of Community*

I have come to you today to say it is so important for you to have connection with your spiritual community.

You have an amazing spiritual community around you, and they can help you move forward in ways you can only imagine. It is time for you to ask for the help of your community. You are fearful about asking for this help as you worry they may think you are not good enough to be in this community. Well, that is far from the truth; you always step in when others ask for help, so why can't you ask?

There is no shame in asking for help; you will be surprised at how many from your community step forward to help you. You will feel so much better, and everything will fall into place. The right people will step forward to help, and you will be able to step forward with ease along your path, so why not ask for that help today?

Affirmation: *It's OK for me to ask my community for help and support now.*

234. SHARK – *Authority*

I have come to you today to say it is time for you to stamp your authority on your business.

You seem to be running your business as a hobby at the moment, and you are wondering why it is not taking off the way you want. This is your time to make a decision on what you truly want.

When you have made that decision, you must put your stamp of authority on it as this will bring a whole new energy into it. For you to do this, you must be 100% clear on what you truly want and start to take the action towards it, as you have just been going with the flow and saying, 'If it happens, it happens,' and this is no way to run your business. You must take the leadership role and take the action, stamp your authority on it, and allow yourself to be the businessperson you can be. Are you in the game or out of the game?

Affirmation: *I place my stamp of authority on my business now.*

235. OCTOPUS – *Master of Disguise*

I have come to you today to say you are the master of disguise.

You have been hiding your true self from everyone, including yourself. You have a disguise for everyone that you meet; you fit into all situations, and you just let others think that they know you, but they don't. It is time to take a hard look at yourself to see who you truly are and allow your true self to emerge.

Yes, it is going to be hard to uncover who you are as you have so many layers around you as a protection, but they are not needed now. You must go in and heal all aspects of yourself, all hidden layers. You have the courage to do this, but you may need a healer, shaman, or mentor to help you go deep within. The first layer will be the hardest, so get the help you need to crack this open. You will soon see your true self emerge.

Affirmation: *I allow my true self to emerge now.*

236. SEAHORSE – *Contented*

I have come to you today to say, you are fully content with life at the moment.

You seem to be very content with life and no matter what you turn your hand to, it all falls into place. What a great feeling it is to be like this and have everything run smoothly. To keep it like this, you must keep yourself grounded daily. Also, on a daily basis, write down what you are grateful for.

We attract what we put out, so keep putting out your energy of contentment and you will keep attracting more of the same. Do not forget your daily practice of gratitude and grounding, as they will keep you in the state of contentment.

Affirmation: *I am full of the energy of contentment.*

237. MOUNTAIN GOAT – *Valuable Lesson*

I have come to you today to say you are in the middle of learning a valuable lesson, or one is on its way.

This is a lesson that you must learn before you can move on to the next level of your soul's path/journey. It is not going to be easy; we have all come here to learn life's lessons, and that is why you have reincarnated at this time.

This lesson keeps showing up time and time again, and you just can't seem to learn from it; every time it comes up again, you say, 'Not again!' but this time is different. You will be going in to heal this on a different level, a much deeper level, as you are a much stronger person; you will finally get that 'a-ha' moment, be able to heal, let it go, and move on.

Affirmation: *I turn my lessons into blessings.*

238. SNAKE – *Primal Energy*

I have come to you today to say you have primal energy available to you.

You have to connect to this primal energy that is available to you at this time. This energy is available to you to heal and expand yourself to your next level of consciousness. As you connect to this energy, it will open up your wild side that is hidden deep within, so you must keep yourself grounded deep within Mother Earth at all times.

You can connect within this energy through chanting, meditation, yoga, breathwork, etc., whichever suits you. It is waiting on you to connect with it. Yes, that strange feeling you have been feeling of late is this primal energy, waiting to connect with you. This will enlighten you as you bring this energy from the base of your spine all the way through your chakra system, clearing, cleaning, and enlightening each one, bringing you to your next level of consciousness. You will be able you use this energy with others to help heal them as this energy will be a part of you.

Affirmation: *I embrace the primal energy that is available to me now.*

239. MONKEY – *Explore*

I have come to you today to say it's time to explore new ideas and ways of being.

You have been feeling that there is so much more out there for you, but you just can't get up and explore. Now is the time for you to start exploring other things. You can try all different things out, and if you don't like it, that's fine; doing it is what is most important, as you will know what works for you and what doesn't.

When you go out to explore, it will bring you a whole new way of looking at life. You will get your drive back and feel more like yourself again, and this will open you up to a whole new way of being and doing, a whole new world. So, what is stopping you from exploring life? Get up and grip it with both hands and enjoy!

Affirmation: *I explore all aspects of life.*

240. SILVERBACK GORILLA – *Dignified*

I have come to you today to say you are a very dignified person.

You hold an air of nobility and self-respect around you, and you are a very fair and kind person. Some people don't get it; they see you as being stuck up, and some feel you are above your station. They say that before they get to know the true you, and sometimes this can get to you.

This is one of those times; you just can't understand how others judge you and speak about you behind your back. It is OK to feel this from time to time, but you should not let them bring you down, as you know who you truly are and how you help others. You always hold that dignified side of yourself, and you never let them see how it affects you. Don't change for anyone; you are who you are, and they can take you for you or not at all.

Affirmation: *I fully accept who I am now.*

241. FAWN – *Innocence*

I have come to you today to say you have a very innocent side to you.

You see the world very differently from others; you see the simplicity of it all, the innocence of it all, and you can also see through others' bullshit. You will always look for the positive in any situation, and you are judged for this. You look at world with childlike wonder, looking for the magic and the innocence. You can't understand how others can be so harsh. You find it hard to be around people like this as it drains your energy, and it can get you very down. The next time you are around people like this, place a protective bubble around you to shield you from this energy; you will see and feel the difference as you will not have taken on their harshness. Do not let others change you or bully you out of your innocence as the world needs people like you.

Affirmation: *I embrace my innocence now.*

242. CAMEL – *Close to Your Chest*

I have come to you today to say you are holding everything close to your chest.

You can't seem to let anything go in case you have a meltdown. You are holding onto hope that it is all going to change for the better. You are afraid to ask or let others know what is really going on. You fear if you say it out loud, you will fall apart, and everyone will see what is really going on.

Now is the time to let it all out and get the help you need. You might need professional help, and that's OK, as this needs to change and change fast before you hit rock bottom. Enough is enough now; you have been dealing with this for some time, and you need help now. Set the wheel in motion and ask. Those close to you know that something is up, but every time they ask, you just shrug it off. But not anymore: this is your time to come clean, and when you do, you will be surprised by how many step up to help, so go ahead and ask now.

Affirmation: *I ask for the help that I need now, and I allow myself to receive it.*

243. GIRAFFE – *Entangled*

I have come to you today to say you are getting yourself entangled in needless things.

You seem to be getting so caught up in other people's business. The reality of it is that it's none of your business, but you can't seem to help yourself as you love the drama. You get so engulfed in the middle of it and wonder why or how this has happened, then you get hurt because you get entangled in it.

This is a pattern for you, and you must look at this as you are starting to lose friendships over it. Stop, step back, ask yourself why you really do it – only you can answer that. The next time things kick off, stop and resist the temptation of getting involved in it. See how it is much better not to be entangled in it, and you can always be there for them and not be involved in the drama.

Affirmation: *I step back, and I don't get involved in the drama.*

244. LEOPARD – *Simplicity*

I have come to you today to say you must bring the energy of simplicity into your life.

You seem to always make life hard for yourself, always second-guessing, not trusting yourself, worrying over nothing, not living in the moment.

You have to move forward from this. It will be hard at times, but you can do it. It will take time; all you can do is trust in yourself and your abilities. There is deep healing to be done, and you will see how these patterns are keeping you from having the life that you want. When you feel yourself overthinking, worrying, etc., flip your thinking to the positive. When you have trust and believe in yourself, life can flow. Now is your time to bring that simplicity into your life. Yes, you can have it all and more – just believe.

Affirmation: *I have the power to create change and bring simplicity into my life now.*

245. RED PANDA – *Tree Wisdom*

I have come to you today to say you have a great connection with the trees.

Have you ever tried to communicate with the trees, felt their energy, hugged one, or felt their magical energy? They are so wise. You have the ability to commune with the trees, and when you do connect with them, they will give you wisdom to share with the world. They will help and direct you along your soul's path/journey. They will bring out your shamanic side that may be hidden from you.

You have heard the whispers of the trees, but you have dismissed them. But not anymore – now is the right time for you to fully connect with them. Call them and see and feel their energy as they share their ancient wisdom with you. Go ahead, embrace your new journey with the tress of wisdom.

Affirmation: *I listen and hear the wisdom of the trees.*

246. WORM – *Dig Deep*

I have come to you today to say it's time to go within and dig deep.

You are going through a transformation at the moment, or you will in the near future. You don't seem to know what end of you is up; this is the stage you are at on your journey. You must go deep within yourself to the depths of your soul to clear, heal, and release. What is holding you back from this transformation? Are you making it harder than it should be? There is an old belief that is rising within you to be released; you must dig deep to leave this pattern or old belief behind you once and for all. You can do this. You have come so far; don't quit just as you reach the finish line. Yes, it can be hard, but you have the strength to dig deep, so don't hold anything back. Don't forget to ask your spiritual team for help as you go through this.

Affirmation: *I dig deep and release all that no longer serves me now.*

247. HIPPO – *Calmness*

I have come to you today to say you bring an energy of calmness with you wherever you go.

You have this beautiful energy of calmness that radiates out of you. Even when there is a crisis or argument, you just seem to be able to calm everyone/thing down; this is an amazing gift that you have. You don't seem to think it's a gift as it comes so naturally to you. Everyone feels this energy off you, but you are unaware of the effect you are having on others. People seem to be attracted to you and this calmness. You must remember to clear and shield your energy as you might be taking others' energy on, or they might be pulling at yours. This is your time to see how this gift you have can help others in times of crisis and not hide it from the world. Trust and believe in your natural ability and allow yourself to shine.

Affirmation: *I accept who I truly am.*

248. PARROT – *Wonder*

I have come to you today to tell you to look and see the wonder around you.

You seem to be only looking at what is wrong, and you can't seem to see the wonder of it all. Take some time to sit outside in nature, or walk in your garden or a park. Listen to the sounds, look at the flowers, the beautiful colours, bees buzzing, birds singing. Just be still and take it all in.

When you do this, you allow yourself to shift from the negative to the positive, and you open yourself up to the small wonders in your everyday life. We can forget when life knocks us off balance, but that's OK. Know that we can come back into balance by opening ourselves up to the wonders of everyday life. Sometimes we just need a little reminder of what is right in front of us.

Affirmation: *I listen to and see the wonders in front of me now.*

249. MEERKAT – *Quick-Witted*

I have come to you today to say. You need to be very quick-witted over the next while.

You will need that aspect of yourself as someone close to you is trying to pull the wool over your eyes. You will be able to see what they are doing, but don't act or say anything. Ask your guides for help, and they will guide you on what to do and say and when. Keep yourself calm and only take action when you're guided to.

Use your gut feelings and guidance, and all will work out for you. This is how you will catch them out, and they will never do this to you again. Don't worry, it will all work out fine; take the action, trust, and believe in divine order.

Affirmation: *I keep my eyes open, and my mouth shut.*

250. PANDA – *Heart Walls*

I have come to you today to say your feelings matter.

You have been hiding your emotional side from everyone, and you keep your true feelings wrapped up inside. You must unwrap these emotions that you have built around your heart as walls, so nobody, not even yourself, could get in at them.

You have so much emotion within these heart walls that you must take them down slowly, so you don't go into a healing crisis. The first wall will be the hardest, and you may need help from a healer, mentor, or shaman for you to release this. Yes, there will be a lot of fear around releasing this, as this is new territory for you. This will open you up to a new way of being; you will let go of the hard exterior and bring that softer side of you out. This will take time, a lot of soul searching, and going deep within, looking at all you have held on to most of your life. Be gentle with yourself and rest when required.

Affirmation: *I allow myself to release all emotion held within me now.*

251. ZEBRA – *Timeout*

I have come to you today to say it's time to reward yourself with some time out.

You have been working so hard lately and looking after everyone. You're feeling a bit stressed at the moment. Now is your time to unwind, do something for yourself, anything that makes you feel good, and put yourself first for a change. You always have some project on the go or are running after your family or helping out friends. You don't give yourself time out. Enough is enough; now is the time to give yourself that much-needed time out.

You're being guided to take this time out to recharge your batteries, to put up your feet, and let others look after you for a change. You must take this rest as it's preparing you for your next level. New ideas can't come in if your mind is busy, so sit back, take the time out, and allow yourself to receive the new ideas that are waiting for you.

Affirmation: *I allow myself time out now.*

252. HEDGEHOG – *Natural Curiosity*

I have come to you today to say you have a natural curiosity for life, and you love to know what is going on.

You just love to know what is going on in your family and friends' lives all the time. Some think you're being nosy, but you're not – you just like to know how they are getting on.

This is your way of showing them how much you care about them. When you meet people for the first time, you tend to ask a lot of questions, and they can be taken aback by this until they get to know you and see that it's just your way and you don't mean any harm. Don't let what they say get to you; you are who you are so just be yourself and they will soon find out you don't mean any harm. Just be you.

Affirmation: *I am me.*

253. OWL – *Presence*

I have come to you today to say it's time you allow your presence to be seen and heard.

You have been sitting in the background of your life for far too long, doing your spiritual work, healing, clearing, and allowing your true divine self to emerge. As you have been doing all this, you have been unlocking your wisdom and knowledge. Now is the time to step out and allow yourself to be fully present in your spirituality. There is no more hiding for you, as you have so much wisdom and knowledge to share with the world.

Now is the time to start a blog or new business, be more active on social media, etc., and allow your presence to be seen and heard. Share your wisdom as there are many waiting to hear. It's part of your soul's journey to share and speak your wisdom. No more hiding – your time is now.

Affirmation: *I am fully present in my spirituality.*

254. BEAR – *Wise Teacher*

I have come to you today to say, you are a very wise teacher.

It is time for you to step into your role as a teacher. You have all the wisdom and knowledge within and you have come through life's lessons.

Now is the time to pull it all in and step into your role. It can be scary as you embark on this journey, but now you have the wisdom to step fully into this.

Take that leap of faith, put out the course or mentorship programme that you have been talking about for some time now. Now is that time to birth this project. You will help so many you are awakening on their path; you will guide and help them along their awakening journey. You have so much to share, allow that wise teacher to emerge now; no holding yourself back anymore, your time is now.

Affirmation: *I step forward into my role as a spiritual teacher/mentor now.*

255. POLAR BEAR – *A Test in Time*

I have come to you today to say you feel like everything you know and believe to be true is being tested at this moment in time.

You're looking and seeing what is wrong with the world and you're seeing past the illusions that are around you. This is having a huge effect on you, and you're finding it hard to cope with it all. Everything around you seems to be false and you're wondering what is real. You're questioning everything you believed to be true, and you're seeing past the conditioning, media, religion, and so on.

What is really going on for you is you're going through a spiritual awakening at this moment in time. You're seeing the world from a very different perspective, and it's like you're truly seeing it for the first time. You need to get yourself a spiritual mentor to help you get through this. They will help you understand what is going on and help you make sense of what you're feeling and seeing. Be gentle with yourself as you go through this awakening.

Affirmation: *I embrace my new way of being and seeing.*

256. SEA LION – *Clues*

I have come to you today to say open yourself up to the clues your guides are sending you.

You have been asking for clues in certain areas of your life, and your guides are sending them to you, but you seem to be missing them. They have sent you a few clues as to what your next steps on your soul's path are. You must put all the clues together as you receive them. You're asking them why they are making the clues so hard for you to pick up. This is a lesson in trust for you. This will show you how to trust the information that you're receiving, they can't just hand it to you. Ask them to make them clearer to you so you can pick up the clues they are leaving for you. Also, open yourself up to receiving; trust and believe in yourself, and all will fall into place.

Affirmation: *I believe in myself; I trust myself.*

257. ANTELOPE – *Happening Quickly*

I have come to you today to say it's all about to happen so quickly.

You have put in all the hard work, the endless clearing and healing, and your life is about to change. This change is about to happen overnight. You have been waiting for this to happen for a long time, and now it's going to happen, but so quickly. Try not to get yourself in a complete tizzy.

You will start to question everything, your ability, your training, your belief, your trust, the whole lot. You may even have a meltdown, and that's OK, it just means you're ready. You can do this, breathe, go within past all the fear and you will see you're ready for this. This is your next step along your journey, so embrace it, don't run away from it. Enjoy your dreams that are about to be fulfilled. Get out of your head in drop into your heart.

Affirmation: *I allow my dreams to be my reality now.*

258. CHAMELEON – *Eyes on the Prize*

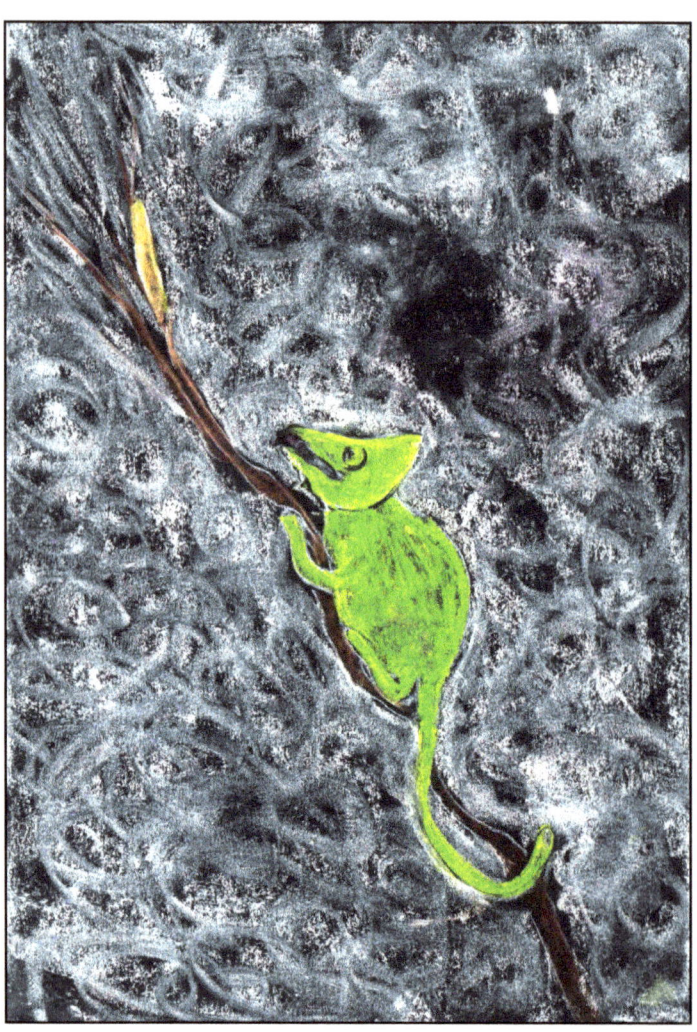

I have come to you today to say keep your eyes on the prize.

Now is not the time to get cold feet or let others talk you out of what you truly want. You have come so far, you have put all the hard work in, and you're nearly at the finish line.

If you give up now, you will regret it for the rest of your life. It's OK to have doubts as you near the end of your journey. You must keep your eye on the prize, this will get you over the finish line. All your hard work is about to pay off, and you will get the recognition you deserve. Let go of other people's opinions and concentrate on what you know to be true. You will get there; believe and trust that you have this in the bag.

Affirmation: *I keep my eye on the prize; I will succeed.*

259. SLOTH – *Be Present*

I have come to you today to say, you need to be present in the now.

You always are ten steps ahead of yourself, and you're not being present in the now. You're letting the beauty of the present moment pass you by. You're always trying to get to the next thing.

You can't live life always pushing onto the next thing, what next, where next. Look at how you're doing this and stop now. The next time you start pushing yourself forward, stop and pause, breathe in and take in all the beauty around you. You will see after doing this that you will have more energy, and you will see how beneficial it's to just stop, pause, and breathe, and how this brings into full balance to your true divine self.

Affirmation: *I stop, pause, and breathe in the beauty around me in this present moment.*

260. DUCK – *Insignificant*

I have come to you today to say let go of the insignificant things you're holding onto.

You're holding onto a lot from your past on a physical and emotional level. Now is the time to let it all go, as they no longer serve you anymore. Holding onto this is not doing you any good. It's keeping you held there, and you can't move forward without releasing this on all levels. You need to journal, heal and release this. It may take you a while to fully release this as you have been holding onto this for a long time. Letting go of the familiar can be hard, and you may need to ask for help – we can all do with help from time to time. Don't worry about others judging you, as we all have our own stories. So, letting go of this insignificant energy will give you a liberating feeling. Go ahead, start today, and set yourself free. There is no time like the present.

Affirmation: *I set myself free now.*

261. DONKEY – *Don't Waver*

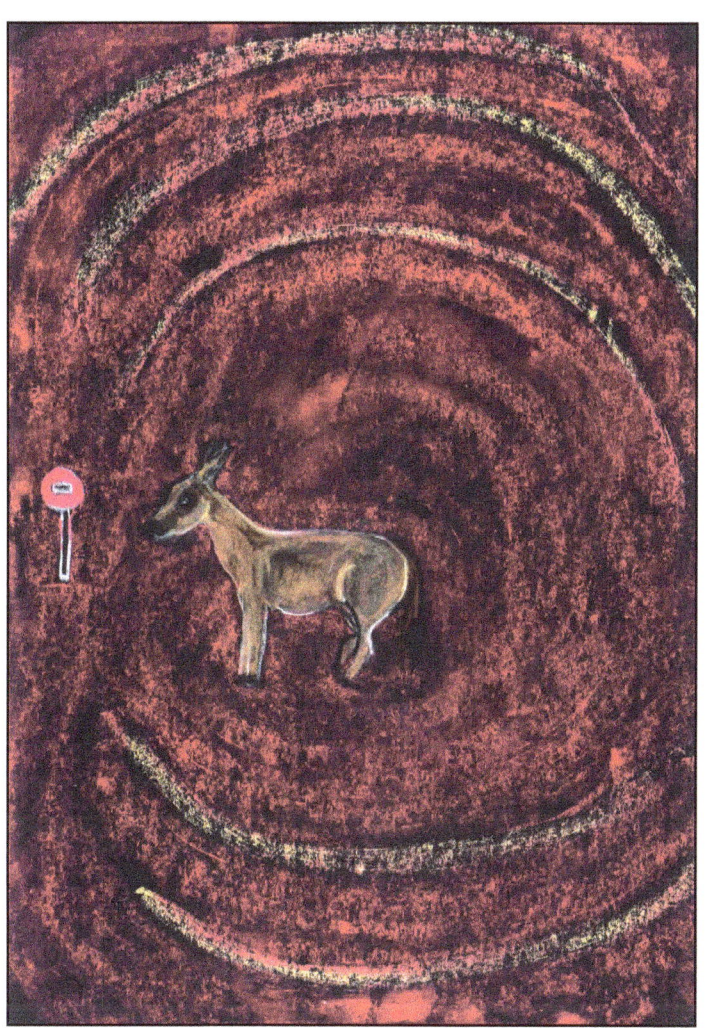

I have come to you today to say do not waver, no matter what.

You must dig deep and not waver on this, you're about to or have had a disagreement with someone, and they want you to change your mind and do what they want. You're quite easy-going and normally just go with the flow.

But not this time – you feel that you did not say or do anything wrong. You also feel that you shouldn't change your mind and it's time that they see things from your perspective and not only theirs. You don't normally mind but this time you do; they are trying to change your mind, but not this time. Don't give in, and stand your ground. It might be hard, but it will be worth it in the end, as they will start to see you for who you truly are. Don't give in.

Affirmation: *I stand my ground with ease.*

262. CRAB – *A Different Approach*

I have come to you today to say it's time to step out of the outcome.

You know what you want in life, and you have a very clear picture in your head. You're using all the manifestation tools and it's still not coming about. You seem to be no closer to your dreams; you're feeling very low at the moment and feel like giving up.

Now is not the right time to give up on your dreams. Keep doing what you're doing on a daily basis, be very precise on every detail, and put a time on when you want to achieve this. Only work on one or two things at once and then step out of the outcome: hand it to the universe and step back. Also, there might be an old belief playing out. We can get so caught up in the outcome that we block it coming to us. So, get out of your own way and allow yourself to receive with ease and flow.

Affirmation: *I sit back and allow my dreams to come to me with ease and flow.*

263. BEE – *Deviation*

I have come to you to say you're very devoted to your work.

You're very devoted to your work and sometimes it leads to others criticising you for this. You can't see why you're like this, and they don't understand you.

This can cause conflict in your relationships, as they feel you don't give them enough of your attention and they feel left out at times. You love and enjoy your work so much that you don't class it as work, but they just can't get their head around this.

Sit down with them and explain the love and enjoyment that your work gives you. You sometimes get so caught up that you forget about them, but it's not intentional. Talk it out and listen to what they have to say and reassure them that you will make more of an effort. Also, make plans to spend time together each week. It's time to bring your life into balance and more flow.

Affirmation: *I bring all aspects of my life into balance.*

264. WASP – *Caution*

I have come to you today to say be cautious over the next few weeks, as all is not what it seems.

Something is going to happen so out of the blue that you will question everything. Be aware of how others are acting around you and how they are reacting to what is being thrown at you, as this is a sign.

Someone you think has your back is going to hang you out to dry. You're going to be very surprised at this. You will be very hurt, feel hard done by, and you will find it hard to forgive them. That's OK. Don't worry, you will get through this; you're stronger than you think. This has happened for you to move forward, as this person was holding you back. You will pick yourself up, you always do; be gentle with yourself as you go through this.

Affirmation: *This too shall pass.*

265. FLY – *A Keen Eye*

I have come to you today to say you have a very keen eye when it comes to new ventures. You know exactly what you want, and you know how to get it. You have a very different way of running your business/life. You get a new idea, and before you know it, you have it up and running; this is a very natural way of doing things for you.

People ask you how you do it and you can't seem to put it in to words, as it's like something inside you activates and you allow it to flow. Others can be a bit critical and spiteful at times; they say you just won't tell them, but they are just jealous of you. Don't allow anyone to stop you; enjoy your gifts and your success. Let yourself fly as high as you can as there is no stopping you now.

Affirmation: *I allow myself to fly high now.*

266. BUTTERFLY – *Navigate*

I have come to you today to say it's time for you to navigate through your transformation.

You have been going through a deep transformation and you're finding it hard to get to the other end. You think you're nearly there but then something else happens. No matter what you do, you just can't seem to get through this and come out the other end. You have so many tools, and everything you need is within you. Look at how and why it's affecting you at this moment and use the tool you need. If you can't navigate through this yourself, think of who you can call on to help at this time.

You will get through this. You're just not seeing what you need to see or learning the lesson. You will. Hang in there and you will soon come out the other end. Be gentle yourself as you go through.

Affirmation: *I allow myself to see and learn the lesson now.*

267. PENGUIN – *Endure Suffering*

I have come to you today to say you don't have to endure this suffering anymore.

You have yourself so caught up in the suffering that it has become a normal way of being and you're asking yourself if this is ever going to end. It will end when you make up your mind to end it, but not until then. Are you ready to let it go? Are you ready to start living your life again? Only you can answer this, nobody else.

You hold the key to unlock the suffering. Only you. It has become so familiar to you that you're fearful about letting it go, fearful of what is next, wondering if you can really be happy. Only you can do this, so get the help that you need and start living the life you want. Do yourself a favour and let go of the suffering. Leave it in the past where it should be.

Affirmation: *I release the energy of suffering and I set myself free.*

268. OSTRICH – *Limitation*

I have come to you today to say stop limiting yourself.

You have a pattern that is running at this time around limiting yourself. You only get so far with everything you have or do and then you limit yourself. You can have it all and more if you allow yourself. You must go within to see how and what is this pattern is about – it can be from a past life, ancestral line, learned beliefs, etc. – and do the healing around it as it must go. It's affecting every area of your life.

Unless you do this, you will never get what you truly want or desire, as you will always have a limit on life and your happiness. Go deep within or get the help you need to clear this pattern once and for all. Switch limited to unlimited. Go ahead, you can do it.

Affirmation: *Yes, I can have it all and more now.*

269. CROCODILE – *Thick-Skinned*

I have come to you today to say you're very thick-skinned.

You have a very thick skin built around you, and this must go, as it no longer serves you. You have years of emotions tucked away that nobody sees, not even yourself. You need to start to let these emotions out one by one; you will not move forward along your path until you do this.

It's going to be hard, but you're well able to do this. You must let down the barriers that you have built. It will take a while to get used to being open to your emotion, but it will be worth every tear along the way, and you have the strength within you to do this. Surrender to these emotions and allow them to go, open your heart, and receive the love. Surrender, release, and receive now.

Affirmation: *I let go of all that no longer serves me now.*

270. EMU – *Victimisation*

I have come to you to say it's time for you to let go of the victim energy that you're carrying.

You seem to be in the energy of 'poor me, look what is happening to me,' and there is always a story about something. You're dragging your energy down every time you step into this, and you're wondering why you can't seem to get out of it. It's like you're loving all the drama and the story.

Yes, things happen that we don't like, but the way you react to it's up to you. You can step into victim mode or look at how you can deal with it; there is always a choice, and that choice is yours. The next time something happens, stop, and make the choice, don't just react. You will soon see the changes, and all will work out. Life will start to flow as you choose to step out of the energy of victimisation. Remember, you always have a choice.

Affirmation: *I let go of the energy of victimisation now.*

271. KANGAROO – *Dreams*

I have come to you today to tell you to keep note of your dreams.

You have been having very vivid dreams, and they don't seem to make sense to you. You're receiving guidance through your dreams, so get yourself a dream journal and write down what you remember of your dream every morning. They will not make sense right now, but they will in the future. They are giving you pieces of the puzzle; you're being guided to look closely at what they are giving you in your dreams.

Trust that in the future they are going to make sense; don't let your mind overthink, as it will all fall into place. Write it all down, even the smallest of details, as it will soon make sense, and your next part of your journey will unfold.

Affirmation: *I trust and believe in the guidance I receive in dream time.*

272. KOALA BEAR – *Appearances*

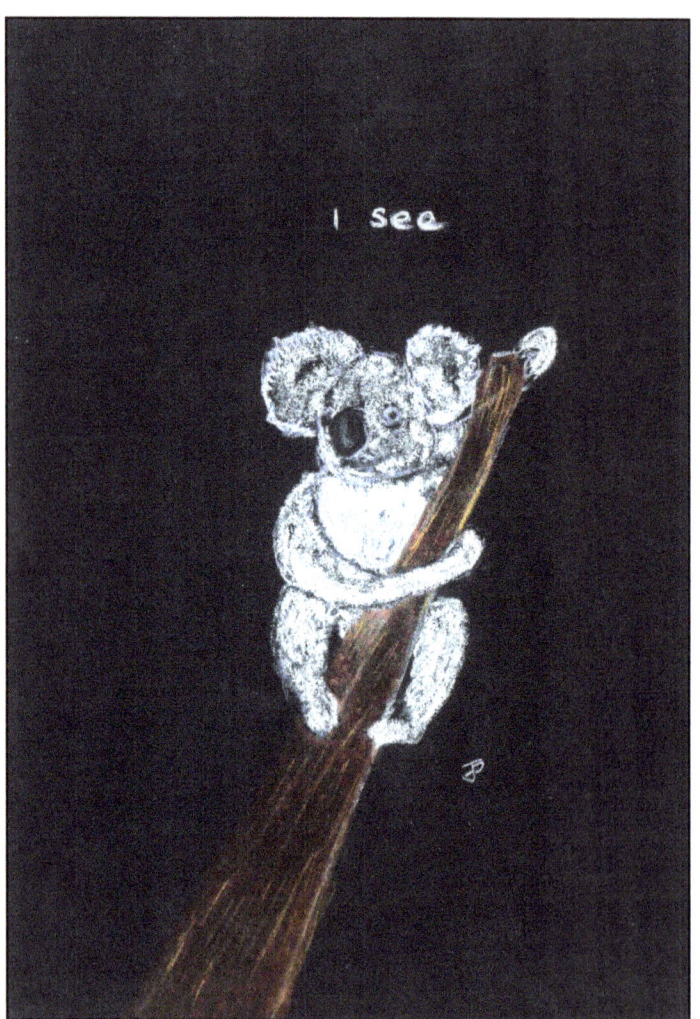

I have come to you today to say don't be fooled by someone's appearance, as they are not what they seem. Don't get sucked into how nice they seem to be. They have a different side to them. There is someone coming into your life that is not very trustworthy. It's someone you know but not very well, but all of a sudden, they are going to want to be your best friend and want to hang out with you.

You might get caught up in it all, and you might even think are they great for helping you. But remember, all is not what it seems, and they have a different agenda running in the background. They are like me, the koala. My coat looks so soft and cuddly, yet it's full of oil. So, don't be fooled, you will soon see them for who they truly are.

Affirmation: *I am not allowing myself to be fooled by others.*

273. PORCUPINE – *Face Your Vulnerabilities*

I have come to you today to say it's time to face your vulnerabilities head-on.

There is no more running away from them. You can be vulnerable when it comes to certain things in your life; being aware of your weaknesses is great insight, as we can do something about them. It can be a hard thing looking at your life through a microscope, as we don't always like what we see. That is why we leave it so long to go deep within, and we allow fear to win.

You have the strength and courage to face this head-on; you want the changes this is going to bring you. This is critical for you to take the next step along your journey. Be brave and face it, you know what needs it be done to move on, and you have the strength and courage within you. There is no holding you back.

Affirmation: *I have the strength and courage to face my vulnerabilities head-on now.*

274. COYOTE – *Fooled Once*

I have come to you today to say you will only be fooled once.

You have been through a difficult time of late, as someone close to you ended up not being what they seemed. You're very hurt over this, and you can't seem to forgive them for their actions. You don't want to go back to get hurt again, but you just can't seem to put it behind you so you can move forward. It's hurting you on a very deep level, and you're heart broken. You can't understand why they did what they did.

They have been asking you for forgiveness, but you just can't go there. You don't want them in your life anymore, as they cut you quite deep. You will get over this but it's going to take time. You will have good days and bad ones. Be gentle with yourself and allow yourself the time and space to heal.

Affirmation: *I give myself the time and space to heal now.*

275. RACOON – Calm Under Pressure

I have come to you today to say you must stay calm under pressure.

You can get quite stressed when you're under pressure, and you don't cope well. You go from 0-100 in half a second, which is not good. You then get yourself into a state and you can't get yourself out of it. You also stress out everyone else around you. Then when you come back to yourself, you're sorry for the way you acted, and you then have to apologise.

This is happening on a frequent basis, and now is the time to do something about it, as you can't keep doing this. The next time you feel the pressure build in you, stop, get up, walk around, do something else, and most of all, breathe. You will feel yourself calming down again. Each time you do this, it will be quicker for you to calm down and you won't fly off the handle. It will get easier with time.

Affirmation: *I keep myself calm under pressure now.*

276. CHEETAH – *Too Many Goals*

I have come to you today to say, you're concentrating on too many goals at one time.

Your concentration is all over the place; you want everything, and you want it now, but it just does not work like that. You must step back and look at what you truly want and be very precise on what that is. You should only work on one or two things at a time. When we focus on too many things, we miss guidance and then you can miss an opportunity to bring your desires to reality – that's why you must focus on two goals max.

I am not saying that you can't have it all – you can, but it will take time and effort, and how quickly that happens is up to you. How much are you willing to do to bring all you want to fruition? It's going to take time and effort. Stop, take time to figure out what you truly want, and go for it.

Affirmation: *I get clear on what my goals are now.*

277. JAGUAR – *Cut Through the Bullshit*

I have come to you today to say it's time to cut through the bullshit and get real. You have so many possibilities and you can't see it. It's like you want it, but you're not fully committed; you want it all to come to you. It doesn't work that way. You must put in the work. You do want the success, but you're telling yourself, 'It will come to me when I am ready.' It doesn't always work that way. You have to take the action, do the work, and then it will come to you.

It won't happen the way you're doing things at the moment. Ask yourself if you really want it, and if the answer is yes, let go of the bullshit you have been telling yourself. Get up, take the action, see how things start to move for you, and you will soon reap the rewards. Now is your time to put up or shut up. Only you can make that choice.

Affirmation: *I let go of the bullshit I am telling myself now.*

278. LYNX – *Paying Attention*

I have come to you today to say you're to pay close attention to what others are saying to you, as there are messages for you within it. Someone is going to suggest that you do something – it will be said as a passing comment, and you might miss it. This is a new way of doing things, and it will bring with it a lot of new possibilities. It will be said in a way that you might miss it, so be very attentive to what others are saying around you.

Keep your ears open and your mind sharp. It will come from the most unlikely person, and they will not repeat it, so be on high alert. You will know straight away when it's said, as it will just sit right with you.

Affirmation: *I am open; I hear what I need to hear now.*

279. OTTER – *What If?*

I have come to you today to ask, 'What if?'

It's time you let life unfold naturally and stop forcing it. You're always caught up in the how, why, and when; you just can't seem to release and let it go. Your mind is like a clock, always ticking. What if …

You're being guided to let life be, no more pushing and shoving. You need this time to allow yourself to relax and take a much-needed break. Let it all go, sit back, allow it to just be, and you will find that when you do this, new ideas and new opportunities will start to come in. They won't when you're pushing and shoving; they will come when you let go of the outcome. When you're in the pushing energy, you're not in the moment, and you're letting life pass you by. When you let go and be, you're in the magic of life. Allow yourself to flow through life.

Affirmation: *I allow flow into my life now.*

280. MOOSE – *Native American Guide*

I have come to you today to say it's time for you to embrace your Native American guide now.

Now is your time to connect with the Native American guide that has stepped forward to help unlock more wisdom within you. You will start to see or hear him/her more clearly. He/she will be guiding you through some meditations that will help you release old patterns and beliefs that you need to let go of before you unlock this wisdom.

Get yourself a notebook and journal every day on what you're experiencing and the guidance you're receiving. He/she is stepping forward at this time because you're ready to embrace this old wisdom and you're ready to bring it to your work through healings. These are old wisdoms that you have used before in a past life; you will find some of it very familiar to you.

Affirmation: *I open myself fully to unlock the wisdom within.*

281. ELK – *Pace Yourself*

I have come to you today to say it's time to pace yourself.

You're always running here and there, and you never give yourself time. You put yourself under too much pressure, always doing and never allowing. This has to stop now.

This is a pattern that is running all the time; you can't seem to change this no matter how hard you try, and you always fall back into the old way of it. Now is the time for you to change this once and for all. Look within and ask yourself why you're running away and what you're trying to avoid. You will get the answer, then you can do the healing. Let it go and allow yourself that much-needed ME time, time just for you. If you're finding it hard to clear this, go get the help that you need. Ask yourself who can help you with this, and trust in the answer. No more running away from yourself – now is the time to pace yourself and allow the healing to occur.

Affirmation: *I pace myself and allow my healing to occur.*

282. HOG – *Stop Waiting*

I have come to you today to say stop waiting.

That time you have been waiting for has gone! You're always saying to yourself, 'I will do that when this, when that,' but you never do it at all, so stop procrastinating and just get on and do it. This is a bad habit of yours, and no matter what, you're always falling back into this pattern. This has to stop once and for all.

You're holding yourself back all the time; now is the time to do the inner work on this and put it to bed. You have great ideas, but you hold them back. Stop blocking yourself from moving forward; you know deep down that you truly want to move forward. The only thing holding you back is you and your beliefs about yourself. No more holding yourself back – now is your time.

Affirmation: *I go deep within and release all that is holding me back.*

283. LIZARD – *What is Your Heart Telling You?*

I have come to you today to ask, what is your heart telling you?

You have a decision that needs to be made and you're finding it hard to make it. You seem to make a decision and then you change your mind minutes later; this is getting you nowhere, so it's time to make that decision and stick to it.

Sit down and take an in-depth look at both sides, make a list of the pros and cons, then tune in to see what is right for you. How does your heart feel when you tune in? That is where you will get your answers. You have felt this feeling before and didn't follow it and that led you down the wrong way, but not this time. Tune into your heart it and you will know what is right for you at this moment in time. Deep down, you know what the decision is, so go ahead and make it.

Affirmation: *I drop into my heart and listen.*

284. SCORPION – Upper Hand

I have come to you today to say you have the upper hand.

You got this. You're about to go after your dreams, and you have full belief in yourself, but others don't. You have listened to the guidance and taken the necessary action to get you this far. Now that you're about to take that leap of faith, others are voicing their opinion, and it's making you uneasy.

Remember, you have the upper hand in this as you have been guided to do what you're doing. Now is your time to bring your dream to fruition. Stop listening to what others have to say; you know deep down it's what you're meant to be doing. Hand them back their projections and fear and allow yourself to be true to you. You're very capable of taking that leap of faith, so go ahead and remember you have the upper hand; you will be guided the whole way through this process.

Affirmation: *I believe and trust in me; I take that leap of faith now.*

285. GOLDFISH – *Pushing Against the Current*

I have come to you today to say stop pushing against the current.

You have a bad habit of pushing against the current when things don't work out your way. You start pushing and looking at other ways of doing it and this causes you to push against the current. It's like you have always been pushing to get where you're going.

It's time to go with the flow of the current, allowing it to carry you, not push against you. Why not try allowing yourself to step back when things don't work out? Maybe they are not meant to. Now is your time to step out of the how, what, and why, and allow life to flow. Let it come to you, rather than you pushing to get it. Life can be so much easier when we do this. Break the old pattern and allow yourself flow and ease.

Affirmation: *I allow myself flow and ease now.*

286. WOMBAT – *Wise Advice*

I have come to you today to say you will be giving some wise advice to someone in the near future.

You're going to be pleasantly surprised as you're going to be asked your opinion on what someone should do. You have so much wisdom within, and it's time to share it and help others.

This person will approach you out of the blue, as they hold you in very high esteem; you're going to be very surprised at who it's. You will feel a bit unsure about it at first, as you don't want them to blame you if things don't work out as they might hang on your every word.

You won't give them bad advice. You will give them your opinion and tell them it's up to them what they do with the advice you gave them, as you feel they should make up their own mind in the end and it will be their decision in the long run. Step out of the overthinking and enjoy being able to help others through your life experiences.

Affirmation: *I allow myself to give advice to others.*

287. CHIPMUNK – *Always Planning Ahead*

I have come to you today to say you're always planning ahead.

Your mind is on overdrive and it's never quiet. You're going to have to quieten the mind to allow the guidance in as it's too busy to allow anything in, and this is holding you back.

Now is the time to look within and see why you're doing this, why you're planning ahead, and why you're keeping yourself busy. What do you not want to face? These are the questions you must ask and go deep within for the answers. You will get the answers by doing the inner work; don't be afraid to do this work – yes, it can be hard, but it's worth it in the end. It's OK to live in the moment. Let go of the planning and just be – life can be so easy if you do.

Affirmation: *It's OK for me to live in the moment.*

288. POSSUM – *Environment*

I have come to you today to ask, are you doing your bit for the environment?

When it comes to helping the environment, every bit helps, big or small. Be aware of how much electricity, gas, and oil you're using, and maybe cut back a little.

Also, make sure you're recycling your plastic, bottles, tins, and food waste. When we do this, we can also save some money on our household bills. You don't have to go to the extreme, just do your bit.

See how much waste you have and how you can cut it down; if we all do our bit, Mother Earth will thank us for it.

Affirmation: *I am at one with Nature and Nature is at one with me.*

289. HYENA – *Be Light of Heart*

I have come to you today to say be light of heart.

You're taking everything that others say to you to heart. You're starting to worry about what others are saying or doing behind your back. You seem to be very on edge at the moment, and nobody can say anything to you, as you take it the wrong way. That is your own stuff coming up to be looked at, not theirs.

You must look at the way this is coming up, what it's showing you and why you're reacting like this. There is something much deeper going on. Journal, meditate, or do what you feel will give you the answer to this. Then clear it, heal it, and allow yourself to be light and not take what others say to heart. Allow your true light-heartedness to emerge and be yourself again.

Affirmation: *I enjoy the lighter side of life now.*

290. CHIMPANZEE – *Act Fast*

I have come to you today to say you have a tendency to act fast and ask questions later.

You have been doing this all your life and it has to stop as it's getting you into all sorts of trouble. You always act before you have the right information, or you get caught up in others' drama, even if it has nothing to do with you, and you wonder why it's happening to you. This has to stop as you have lost a lot of friends over the years from doing this.

The next time something happens, stop and assess the situation before you act – or better still, don't act at all. Just allows it to unfold with no input. It will take time for you not to react when things are going on, but the most important part is that you're aware of what you're doing. Soon you'll be able to not react at all. You always have a choice.

Affirmation: *I stop and assess the situation before I act now.*

291. JELLYFISH – *Take Everything in Stride*

I have come to you today to say take it all in stride.

Look at how you're getting caught up in everything. You seem to be tangled in a lot, and you have so much going on. Now is the time to take a step back and take everything in stride. You're going to find it hard to do this as you're so used to doing it all. You never seem to give yourself time to sit back and take the load off.

Dig deep, set that carefree attitude loose, and let it back into your life. Now is the time for you to get out of your own way; you're making things complicated that don't need to be. Drop into your heart and ground. Be like me, the jellyfish, and let life's tide guide you and carry you for a while. Yes, you can do this.

Affirmation: *I allow the tide of life to carry me for a while.*

292. SQUIRREL – *Better Days Ahead*

I have come to you today to say there are better days ahead for you.

You have been going through a tough time lately and you can't seem to get back to ease and flow. Every time you think you're getting this ease back, something else happens. You feel like you can't take much more, and you have had enough. Be careful with your words – what you're saying is, 'I don't want this, I am sick of this,' and this is what you're attracting at the moment. You're a powerful manifestor, so be careful of what you're saying.

When you catch yourself saying something you don't want, right away, say, 'Cancel, clear, delete,' then say something positive you want to bring in. Say it with emotion and as if you already have it. Example: 'My life is very simple and easy.' You will be surprised how quickly you can change your life.

Affirmation: *My life is very simple and easy.*

293. BAT – *Deep-Rooted Fears*

I have come to you to say you have very deep-rooted fears, and they are holding you back. You have them buried so deep that you can't see even see them, or you just don't want to. You're going to need the help of a shaman, healer, or mentor to release these. You have been avoiding these for years; you have been scratching the surface of them and pushing them further down, but not anymore.

The time has come to face them head-on. Yes, it's going to be hard, but not as hard as not facing them. You will come out the other end as a much stronger person. Now is your right time to do this, so make that call and set the wheels in motion.

Affirmation: *I have the strength and courage to face my deep-rooted fears now.*

294. HARE – *Spring Clean*

I have come to you today to say, it's time for a spring clean.

No matter what season you're in, you can always spring clean. Look at your home first and see what needs to be cleared. Get rid of old, broken, or unwanted things you have lying around. Get into the back of the presses, wardrobes, drawers etc., and give your home a good declutter and clean. You can do the same in your office or workspace.

As you do this, you will feel so much lighter, as everything we hold on to has energy and we can't bring in the new if our space is full of things we don't use or want. This will open you up to a whole new energy that has been waiting for you, as it couldn't come in if there was no space for it. You must do this physical decluttering and clearing at least three times a year. Remember to use sage to clear your space of negative energy and allow the positive energy in. Embrace all the new energy that awaits you.

Affirmation: *I am open to new energy that awaits me now.*

295. FROG – *Cleansing Through Water*

I have come to you today to say you will need to do a cleansing through water.

You're holding onto a lot– old patterns, paradigms, etc. – and it needs to go. This has all resurfaced over the past while and you're saying to yourself, 'I have dealt with this before, oh no, not again.' This has come back up and bit you in the ass and knocked you off-centre. You can't seem to shift it this time.

For you to shift this, you must do a ritual by cleansing with water. Get into the bath if you can, light candles, use Epsom salts, then set your intention to release all that needs to be released. (If you don't have a bath, get into the sea, as it will have the same effect.) As you immerse yourself in the bath, repeat three times, 'I release all that is holding me back, knowing and unknowing, hidden and deeply hidden, through all time and space, multi-dimensional, through all lifetimes. I request this three times. So it should be and so it is.' You may need to repeat this clearing through water a few times over the next week, as each time it will release another layer.

Affirmation: *I release all that is holding me back, knowing and unknowing, hidden and deeply hidden, through all time and space, multi-dimensional, through all lifetimes. I request this three times. So it should be and so it is.*

296. MOLE – *Connecting with Earth's Rhythm*

I have come to you today to say you must connect in with Earth's rhythm.

There is so much healing with Mother Earth and you have the ability to connect with the rhythm, to bring this energy through and use it to help heal yourself and others. You have a great connection with Mother Earth, and she with you. She has been calling you for a while now, you just haven't heard her, or you weren't sure why she was calling you.

Now you know, so connect in with her and she will show you how to connect with her properly to bring in the rhythm of Earth fully. She will teach you how to use these energies to heal yourself first and then to help you heal others. This energy will open you up to a whole new way of being and doing. Get out of your head and drop onto your heart, and allow yourself to embrace this new rhythm of Earth as there are exciting times ahead for you.

Affirmation: *I fully connect and embrace the rhythm of Mother Earth now.*

297. ANT – *Organised*

I have come to you today to say it's time to get organised in all areas of your life.

You must get organised; you seem to be all over the place at the moment and can't seem to get anything done. It's time to look at what you're holding onto on a physical level, letting go of the mess around you. Get your space cleared and calm, as there is a heaviness around you that is affecting you on all levels.

Start by organising your space and then grounding yourself. Do a deep clearing of your space; don't forget to go deep down into the ground below your space as this important, then do energetic clearing on yourself. You will start to feel so much better after this, and you will be able to be more organised as you will not be carrying others' energy. Remember to do this every time you feel yourself becoming unorganised, or do it once a week; allow it to become a habit for you as it will serve you well and keep you organised.

Affirmation: *I let of the mess, and I organise myself and my space.*

298. BEETLE – *Take Responsibility*

I have come to you today to say it's time for you to take responsibility for your own actions and decisions. Stop passing everything onto others, and sort your own mess out. You always hand the responsibility over to others when things go wrong for you, and you give them a guilt trip if they don't sort it out for you. Not anymore – you have to do it for yourself now.

You aren't doing yourself any favours by doing this, and you're only making life harder for yourself in the long run. The next time something goes wrong for you, stand on your own two feet and sort it out yourself; if you don't, someday there won't be anyone to pick you up. So, stand on your own two feet and take responsibility for yourself. You will feel so much better in yourself by controlling your own life.

Affirmation: *I take responsibility for my own actions now.*

299. DRAGONFLY – *Habits That Need to Change*

I have come to you today to say you have a habit that needs to change. You have had this habit most of your life, and it needs to stop. It's your go-to when things get stressful and uneasy, but it's not good for you, and you know this. You're ready to make this change and it will be for the better.

The next time you get stressed and feel yourself going into this, ask yourself the question, 'How do I change this?' Listen to the answer. It's not going to be easy to change this, but you will get there with time, so go easy on yourself as you have had this running in you for most of your life. Believe in yourself, and all will work out. Yes, you can overcome this.

Affirmation: *I release this old habit with ease now.*

300. HUMMINGBIRD – *Seek Guidance*

I have come to you today to tell you to seek guidance.

There is something that you want to change or there is something on your mind, and you just can't seem to get to the bottom of it, but that's OK. Sometimes we can't do it on our own, and we need help from others. Now is that time for you to go and seek guidance from someone you can trust to help you through this. You have a lot of friends in the spiritual community, but you're not sure who can help.

Sit with your guides and ask them to bring forward the person who can help you, then get in touch. You will start to feel so much better once the wheels are in motion. This person will help you change what needs to be changed and bring you back into alignment with your true divine self. So go ahead and get the guidance you need now.

Affirmation: *I seek wise council now.*

301. TORTOISE – *Carrying Too Much*

I have come to you today to say stop carrying everyone else's crap on your shoulders.

You have been taking on everyone else's crap along with your own and carrying it around with you every day. Enough is enough now. You're carrying an energetic bag full of crap around with you all the time, so it's no wonder you're feeling tired and weary all the time. Now it the time to let it all go – this has to stop.

Be like me, the tortoise – retreat within and meditate, and give everyone back their stuff. Cut the cords, take back your power with pure love, ground and clear your energy, and place a shield around you. You must do this every day for a week then every third day for another week, then once a week. You will start to feel so much better after you do this. Check in with yourself and make sure you're not carrying others' crap, as this does not serve you well.

Affirmation: *I reclaim my power with pure love and light now.*

302. SNAIL – *Use Your Time Wisely*

I have come to you today to tell you to use your time wisely.

You always get yourself caught up in worrying about how much time you have, but you have all the time in the world if you use it wisely. Now is your time to make a much-needed plan of action and set yourself proper time to get things done. You seem to start something and get distracted and go off and start something else, and then you start saying, 'I don't have time to finish this or that.' Ask yourself why this is happening and why you can't seem to complete the task at hand. How can you change this?

Prioritise what needs to be finished and give yourself the appropriate time to finish it, then you will not get caught up with the time and it will flow with ease. You can see the pattern now, so it's time to do something about it. Make yourself a time-management plan and stick to it, then you will have all the time in the world to do all you want to.

Affirmation: *I plan my time wisely now.*

303. SWAN – *Upper Limits*

I have come to you today to say it's time to break your upper limits.

You have put a limit on yourself as to how much you can achieve, but now is the time to break through that limit. There should be no limit to what you can achieve in your life and this old belief has to go now. You have come full circle in what you have set out to achieve on your path. You never thought in your wildest dreams that you would achieve all you have done. Well, you have.

Now you must set new goals and new dreams, yet you seem to be holding yourself back. Look and see how far you have come, what you have achieved, and know you can achieve anything you put your mind to. Let go of the limits as there is no limit on what you can do and have, so break and release and heal that old belief, and set your sights to the highest that you can, as you can have it all and more. No more limits.

Affirmation: *I release all limiting beliefs now; I have no upper limits.*

304. WOODPECKER – *Door Open Wide*

I have come to you today to say there is a door open wide for you now.

You can't seem to see the door that is wide open in front of you. It's like your eyes are shut and you just can't seem to see it. Open your eyes and see what is straight in front of you. You are so caught up in the negative that you can't see the positive in front of you. You have been asking for the door to open, and it's right in front of you, but you just can't see it. Sometimes when we are looking for change, we focus on what we think it should look like, but in fact, it's something very different or so simple that we can't see it.

You're being asked to trust and follow the sign that you see, no matter what it is. Follow it and when you get that guidance, just do it, no questions asked. This will bring you through that open door. The change you seek so much is waiting for you as you walk through the doors – no looking back, only look to the future as that is where exciting times await you. Are you ready to see what is right in front of you? It's time to trust and allow.

Affirmation: *I trust and see what is in front of me; I step through the open door now.*

305. SALMON – *Travel*

I have come to you today to tell you to pack your bags, as you're about to start travelling.

You love to travel, and you can be quite adventurous. You're about to embark on a journey of a lifetime. You have been talking about this for some time now, how you would love to travel to this place, and you have even imagined what it would be like. The only thing that has been holding you back is the money. Not anymore.

Don't worry about how you're going to get the money; all you have to do is start making the plans, pick the date, who you're going with, and for how long. It's your destiny for you to travel here, as you will be going through a huge awakening when you get there. This is a soul a calling. Let go of thinking, 'I haven't got this or that.' Trust that all will fall into place as this trip is a soul destiny trip. Just allow.

Affirmation: *I trust all will fall into place as it's divine timing.*

306. CROW – *Powerful Foresight*

I have come to you today to say you have powerful foresight, and you dismiss it a lot of the time. You see things and then they come true. You often say to yourself, 'I saw that before it happened!' This has been happening to you for a while now, but you're fearful about telling others as they might think you're mad! You don't trust and believe in yourself to pass on the information you're receiving, and you have a tendency to not say anything when this happens.

It's time to start believing in yourself and use your gifts. Don't worry about what other may think, as this is a gift that can help and guide others along their paths. No more holding yourself back; you must pass on the information as you get it, no matter how it may sound, as it will always resonate with the person you're giving it to. Allow your gift of foresight to unfold, and you will be surprised how your life will change. Exciting times lie ahead if you allow yourself to unlock your true soul's path.

Affirmation: *I allow my gift to expand; I trust and believe in myself now.*

307. DOG – *Sociable*

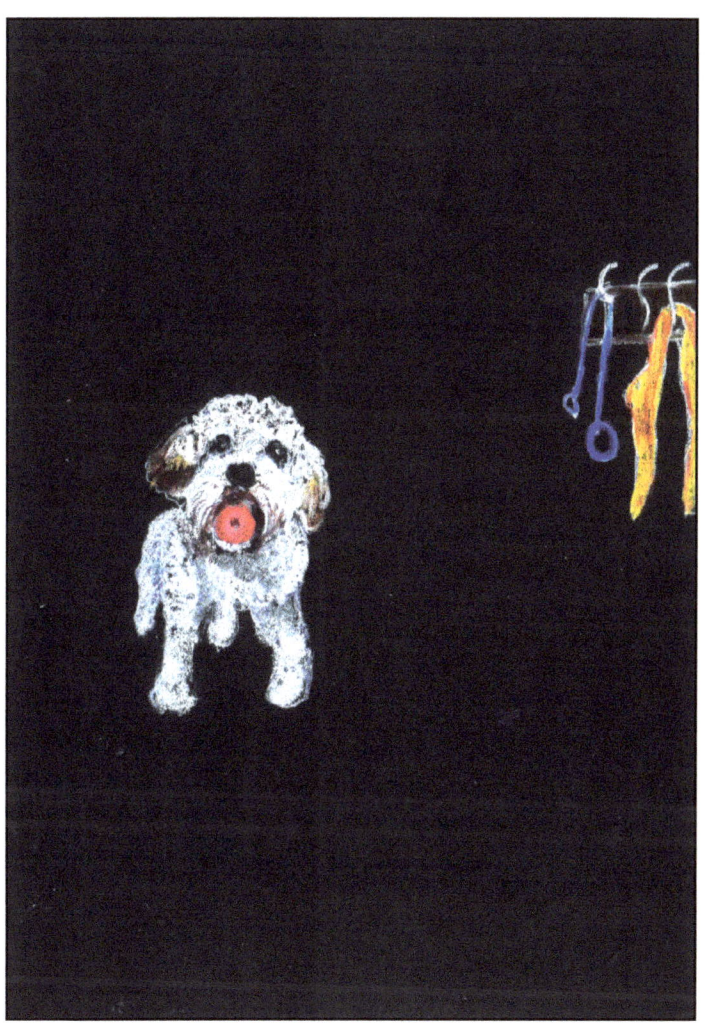

I have come to you today to say it's time to be more sociable.

You need time out to enjoy life a little, meet up with friends, and have a good old natter. You're always working or looking for the next new project, and you don't make time for friends or just going out for some fun. When was the last time you went on a night out, met up with friends, went to the cinema or out for a bite to eat? Yes, it's that long you can't remember.

Now is the time to pick up the phone and arrange a time to go out and let your hair down. No more making excuses as you will be surprised how much you will enjoy it. So, make that call, reconnect, and have some fun – you deserve this time out with friends.

Affirmation: *I allow myself time to be sociable now.*

308. CAT – *Reassurance*

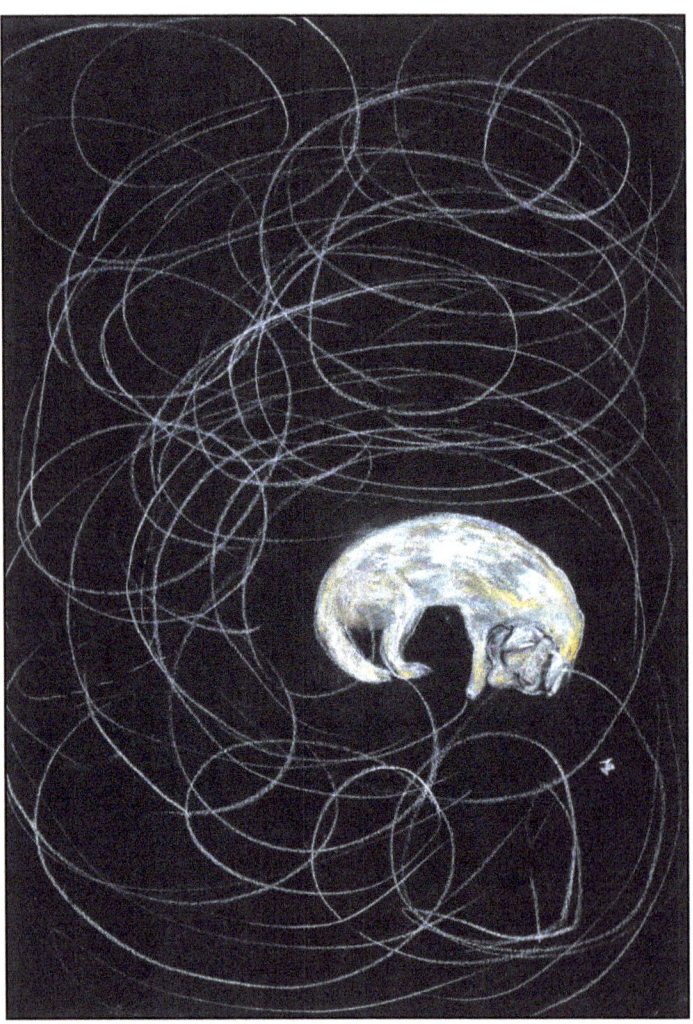

I have come to you today to give you some reassurance that everything will be OK.

You're going around in circles at the moment, and you have been asking when this is all going to end. You can't see to get out of this situation you're in. Every time you try, something else pulls you back in and down. You are on the point of breaking.

I am here to reassure you that all is going to be clear for you; you just need to hang a little bit longer, as your guides are working away in the background, but you just can't see it. Divine timing has to come into play with this, so hold your faith, trust, and all will be OK in the end. There is so much change in the near future for you, and a little while longer is not going to kill you – so hang on, and all will be revealed soon.

Affirmation: *All will work out in divine timing.*

309. HORSE – *Competitive*

I have come to you today to say you're very competitive in everything you do.

Sometimes this competitiveness is a good thing, but other times it's not so good. You don't like to lose; you always want to be the best, and you push yourself to be the best always. You push yourself hard, which is not good. Life is about ease and flow, not to push and shove. You don't have to compete in everything in life.

You need to look at the areas that are most affected by this competitive side to you. You need to heal and release, let go and surrender, as this energy is not good for you anymore and no longer serves you. Now is the time to get the flow and ease in your life, and allow it all to fall into place. Let go of that competitive nature of yours, and surrender to ease and flow.

Affirmation: *I let go of my competitive side.*

310. MOUSE – *Stay on Track*

I have come to you today to say it's time for you to stay on track.

Stop putting your attention on other things when you must keep yourself on one track for the moment – it will be worth it in the end. You seem to be looking at what everyone else is doing, and this is pulling you off your own track. You're getting distracted by wondering how they are doing and how further you think they are than you. You must let this all go and concentrate on yourself and what you need to be doing. Otherwise, you'll feel you're getting nowhere.

Now is the time to focus on yourself and what you're doing, and put all your energy into yourself. Make a list of what you need to do and stay on track. You're doing great, and you have come so far – just remember that the next time your concentration wavers a bit. Pull yourself back in and stay on track, and you will achieve all you want to. Believe in yourself and your abilities; you have come so far.

Affirmation: *When I stay on track, I achieve all I want to achieve.*

311. RABBIT – *Lucky Charm*

I have come to you today to say I am your lucky charm.

Your luck is about to change: you're going to win money, have a debt paid back, or receive a wage increase or new clients. Yes, prosperity is coming to you now. You have been struggling for a while, with too much outgoing and not much money coming in. That is about to change for you. We have heard your prayers and they are going to be answered.

Life is about to get so much easier for you now. You're going to be able to pay off your debt, and this will bring you the much-wanted final freedom you have been craving for some time now. Don't get caught up in the how – just allow, it's on the way. Yes, I am your lucky charm.

Affirmation: *I am financially free now.*

312. SPIDER – *Clear Path*

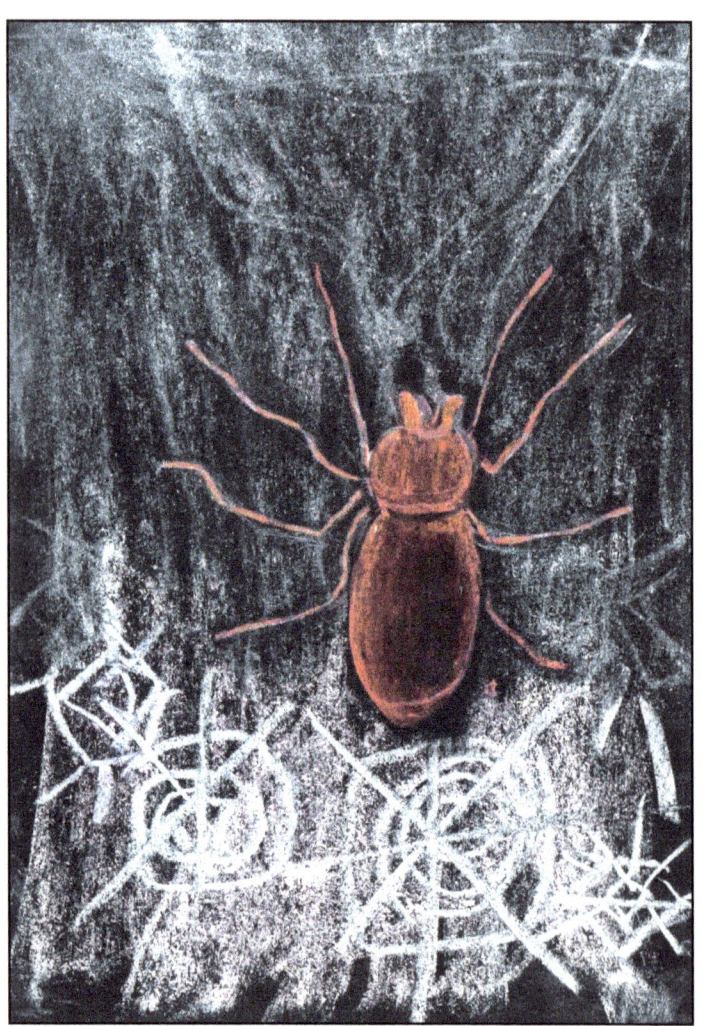

I have come to you today to say the path is clear.

Now is your time to step out and be seen. Allow your dreams to come true; you have been waiting for a sign, and this is that sign. Now is your time, no holding back. Yes, your path is clear. Go ahead and make that move. There is no time like the present to step out and take that leap of faith.

Your path is clear, there is nothing to hold you back, and there are no hidden obstacles. Be like me, the spider, and weave your own destiny. What are you waiting for you? You have been given the go-ahead. Make that move and dream big as it's all there waiting to happen. Go ahead, weave that web of destiny now, your path is clear.

Affirmation: *My path is clear; I weave my own destiny.*

313. FOX – *Sense of Humour*

I have come to you today to say you have a great sense of humour and you don't let life get you down. This is a great quality to have. You always look at the bright side of life, no matter what is going on. Don't let others mock you for this, this is who you are. You have a very different way of looking at life, and it gets you through the good times and the bad times.

When others come to you, you give them advice. They get so much out of the way you see things; you also think outside of the box when looking at a situation, and you can see where it needs to change. Don't let others knock you for this; this is who you are, so don't change for anyone.

Affirmation: *I am who I am.*

314. WHITE STAG – *Air Element*

I have come to you today to say you have a connection with the element of air.

You have a very original way of doing things, you're very passionate about what you do, and you have vast knowledge. This all comes from the element of air, and it has so much more to teach you. Now is your time for you to fully connect with this element. You will be able to harness this energy for healing yourself and others; it has great wisdom to share with you.

The next time you're out, sit and listen to the wind. Truly listen as it will speak to you, it will give you direction, and it will teach you. You will find a way to fully connect and trust this element of air. Use the energy to help you breeze through life, as it will help clear away the fog and obstacles in life and give you a clear path. What are you waiting for? Embrace the element of air – it's all around you.

Affirmation: *I embrace the element of air now.*

315. WOLF – *Make Your Position Known*

I have come to you today to tell you to make your position known.

You have been hurt by someone close to you and they have no idea that they hurt you. They are going about their life as if nothing happened, and they are unaware of what they have done to you or how it's affecting you. Enough is enough: you must let them know how they hurt you.

Sit down with them and let them know how and why you're feeling this way, as they can't do anything about it if they are unaware of what they did. They will be very surprised that they hurt you, as this was not their intention. Let them explain why they did what they did, and you will see it was not intentional. Do yourself a favour and have that chat, and clear the air before it gets out of hand on your part. They can't do anything about it if they don't know they hurt you.

Affirmation: *It's OK to make my position known.*

316. COW – *Relish Stability*

I have come to you today to say you're relishing your stability at the moment.

It seems to be the only thing on your mind right now; you have been longing for this for a while, and it's finally here. Life has dealt you a rocky road up to this point, and now you're ready to settle down and allow stability into your life.

You want to just go with the flow, easy does it, and not get too caught up in life's ups and downs. You're done with the drama. Think long and hard, and think your decisions out. This will help you bring stability into your life and allow you to stay in that ease and flow. You may be letting go of old friends as you don't want the drama that is attached to their lives, and that's OK. We can all move on in life, so let go of the guilt when it happens. The only thing you must concentrate on is the ease and flow you want in your life, then relish the stability you have so longed for.

Affirmation: *I relish the stability in my life now.*

317. BLACK SHEEP – *Sheeple*

I have come to you today to say, don't be a sheeple (someone who just follows the herd). Step out of the crowd, stop listening to the media, and make your own mind up. You seem to be following the crowd the moment, but you know deep down that this is not your truth. But fear and control have a grip on you at the moment, as you're listening and watching too much of it.

You know deep down what is right for you, so don't let others' opinions and judgement take hold of you. Call all your energy back, stop listening to the media, ground and come back into your true self. Then you will see it very differently. You will see what is really going on. Sometimes you feel you don't fit in and that you're not accepted for what you believe in. Self-acceptance is the most important thing; don't let others try to change you. You are who you are. It's OK to be different and not follow the crowd. Be yourself, believe in yourself, and be true to you.

Affirmation: *I accept myself for who I truly am.*

318. BADGER – *Seek Solitude*

I have come to you today to say you seek solitude at the moment.

You just want to be left alone right now and others just can't seem to get that. You're at a crossroads in life, and you're unsure of which way to go or what path to take. For you to make this decision, you must retreat within. You need to explain how you're feeling and why you're feeling like this to others, and they will give you that solitude that you desire.

Take a few days away by yourself in a quiet place and stay away from your phone, then sit and make that much-needed decision on what path/direction you want to take. This is an important decision that you're about to make, so take as much time as you need as it will affect the rest of your life. Retreat to the solitude that you so desire, and take all the time and space you need.

Affirmation: *I retreat within to make my decision with ease now.*

319. ROBIN – *Turning a Blind Eye*

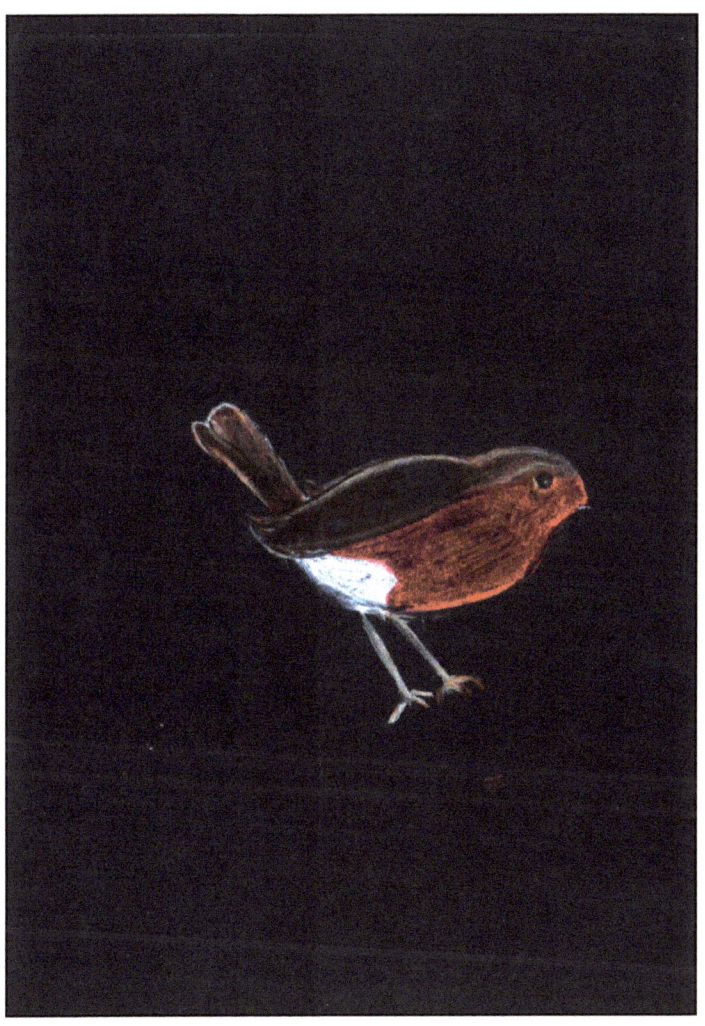

I have come to you today to say stop turning a blind eye.

You have been doing this for quite a while and not confronting the problem at hand. You're hoping it will go away by itself and you won't have to deal with it. That is not the case; you're going to have to deal with this once and for all, as if you don't, it will keep tripping you up until you do. No time like the present. You have tried to deal with this before and you went so far, but you were finding it too hard, and so you just left it – but not this time.

This time, it has to be dealt with once and for all, as you will not be able to move forward without dealing within this. So do what has to be done; yes, you know what that is. No more running away from it, no more turning a blind eye – that won't help you anymore. This will show you how strong you truly are.

Affirmation: *I face my challenges head-on.*

320. EAGLE – *Personal Freedom*

I have come to you today to say, you're nearly there – personal freedom is about to be yours.

You have been looking for the freedom to be yourself, without others criticising you or projecting onto you. You have done a lot of inner work on this, and you're nearly there. You're done with what others think of you, and you're feeling that sense of freedom to be you.

It has been a long road to get here, but worth every bit of it; life will start to get easier for you, and you will find your tribe. When you do, you will feel that sense of personal freedom. No one will be able to take your power again as you will have a sense of belonging to you and that personal freedom to be yourself. Enjoy this newfound freedom and look at how far you have come and how much you have achieved along the way. Congratulations, you did it!

Affirmation: *I am free to be myself now.*

321. BLACKBIRD – *Values*

I have come to you today to ask, what are your core values?

How important are your values to you? Are you going to let yourself down by allowing others to treat you the way they are or behave in a way that does not sit with your core values? Are you being influenced by others? Whatever their core values are, they don't seem to meet yours. This is not your way of doing things; you don't just use others to get what you want, at whatever cost.

You're better than this; you're not normally easily led by others. Normally, you speak your truth and don't waver from your values. Look and see why this person is having such a big impact on your life, before it's too late. Don't change for anyone. You are who you are, and you have very good values.

Affirmation: *My core values are very important to me; I am who I am.*

322. WEASEL – *Intervention*

I have come to you today to say it's time for an intervention.

There is someone around you that needs you to intervene before it's too late. They really need your help, but they just can't seem to ask you for it. You have helped this person before, but to no avail, and they are afraid to ask you again.

You're saying to yourself, 'Why should I? I have helped before, but it didn't work.' They were not ready the last time, but they are ready now for help. You know what they need and where they need to go. Believe it or not, your opinion matters to them a lot. Yes, it can be hard going back again, but you know deep down that it will work out this time. They will get themselves sorted, once and for all, with your help. Go ahead and do what you know needs to be done. Intervene before it's too late

Affirmation: *I hold my faith and trust all will work out now.*

323. BUFFALO – *Stay True to Yourself*

I have come to you today to say stay true to yourself, no matter what. Someone is going to try and get you to question who you truly are. They are going to do this to get you out of the way so they can get what they want. They want what you have, and they will do whatever it takes to get it. Be on your guard as this is someone you would never think of to do such a thing. They will use anything to knock you down and discredit you and your beliefs. They have been plotting behind your back for some time now.

Be on your guard, keep yourself grounded, and question what others are doing around you. You're more powerful than this person. They have done it before and gotten away with it, but not this time, as they have met their match. No matter what is going on, be true to yourself and your beliefs. Take this as one of your lessons in life and learn from it. You will get through this once you hold your faith and be true to yourself.

Affirmation: *I hold firm and stay true to myself no matter what.*

324. ELEPHANT – *Seek Harmony*

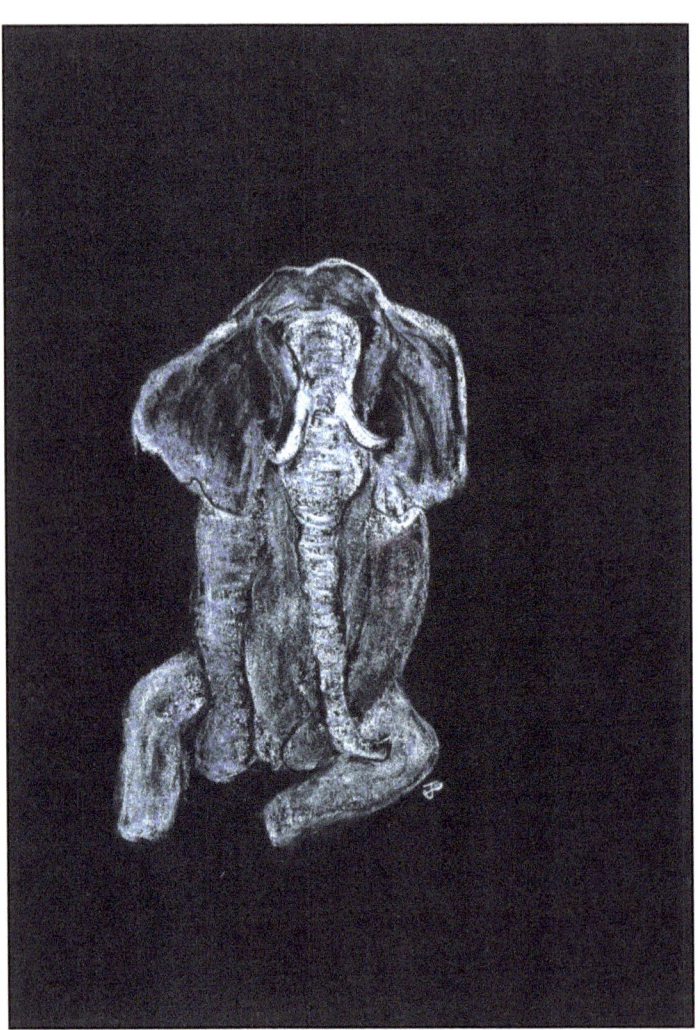

I have come to you today to ask, are you seeking harmony within your family and tribe?

There has been a bit of conflict within your family/tribe. You want to bring the harmony back in, but you can't seem to get everyone to forgive and move on. It's upsetting you that you can't solve this. This is the first time that this has happened on this level, and you're finding it hard to make peace with it. Every time you get them all together, it starts all over again. You feel you're caught in the middle of it, and you can see both sides of it, but you're not willing to take either side.

For this to be resolved, they must forgive each other, and then they will make amends with each other. You must take a step back and allow them to resolve it themselves; otherwise, they will blame you, and that will make matters worse. Step out, set your intention, trust and believe that all will work out in divine timing. That's all you can do; harmony will be restored in time, so hold your faith.

Affirmation: *I believe and trust all will work out in divine timing.*

325. LION – *Let Your Wild Side Out*

I have come to you today to tell you to let your wild side out. You have a wild side of you that is wanting to come out. You don't like to let it out as this side of you can be unpredictable. You don't show that side of you to anyone, as you're afraid of what you could get up to.

You need to let it out – what's the worst that can happen? You go a bit wild, do something out of the normal and fun. You need to do this and allow yourself to be free; no more hiding this side of you. Set your fear aside and enjoy your life. So what if others judge you? That's their stuff, not yours. They are only jealous of you because they would love to do it themselves, but they don't have the confidence within themselves to let themselves free. Set yourself free, be yourself, let that wild side out, and embrace it.

Affirmation: *I set myself free to be me.*

326. TIGER – *Rash Decisions*

I have come to you today to say don't make any rash decisions.

You have a tendency to make decisions without thinking them through properly, and this can cause you trouble from time to time. Now is one of those times not to make rash decisions. Allow yourself to sit with the choice at hand, and look at each decision or path and where it will lead you. Make a list of the pros and cons. Do some homework, and look more deeply into it.

Don't make your mind up until you have all of the above done; when you have it done, meditate and seek guidance on it. Allow your intuitive side to help and guide you, as it will never leave you astray. When you have done all this then you can make your decision; it will be the right one for you, and you won't have any regrets.

Affirmation: *I look and see what the right decision is for me now.*

327. RHINO – *Seeing Lack*

I have come to you today to ask, are you seeing lack around you?

You're looking around you and all you see is what you don't have, what you lack. You're moaning about not having this and that, and you're holding yourself in this energy of lack. Stop, open your eyes, and see all you do have – your home, car, job, business, family, friends, holiday, etc. – and feel gratitude for it all.

The more we get caught up in the energy of lack, the more we attract. So, stop looking at the negative, and start practicing gratitude. Start putting your energy into the gratitude and see how life will change; those things you wanted when you were in the energy of lack will become a reality. Energy flows where your attention goes, so put your energy into gratitude.

Affirmation: *I let go of lack and I embrace the abundance around me now.*

328. LADYBIRD – *Remedies*

I have come to you today to say now is your time to take a course on natural remedies.

You have been looking for something new, a change, and now is your opportunity. You must unlock the wisdom within you; it needs to be unleashed and by doing a natural remedies course, this will happen.

You have had a past life working with herbs, creating remedies. Now is the time to unlock that wisdom that you hold within. This will come naturally to you when you start doing it, and this will be the start of awakening for you. You will be opening yourself up to a new way of being and working. All is about to change and bring you new beginnings in all areas of your life. There is no time like the present, so go book that course and embrace the new opportunities coming your way.

Affirmation: *I allow my natural gifts to unfold.*

329. HAMSTER – *Be Mindful of Your Health*

I have come to you today to say be mindful of your health. You may be feeling under the weather, but you keep telling yourself it will pass. You have been saying this for a while now. Now is your time to go and get it checked by your doctor or seek medical advice on it. Get that check-up and put your mind at ease. There might be a slight adjustment that you need in order to get yourself feeling fit again.

Don't delay; get yourself checked out and sorted so you can get on with the rest of your life, as behind it all you're really starting to worry and are a bit fearful. It will all work out fine. Make that appointment today.

Affirmation: *I listen to my body, and I take the necessary action now.*

330. RAT – *Uncertain Steps Forward*

I have come to you today to say it's OK to take the uncertain steps forward.

You're unsure of what the future holds for you if you go down one path but are unsure where it will lead you. You're being called to follow this path, but you can't see a clear way forward; this is really shaking you and bringing up all sorts of fear.

Sometimes when we follow our instinct, we are unsure where it's brought us. Yet deep down we know that this is the right path for us. You know deep down you should be doing this, but the fear is knocking you off balance, and you're questioning everything you know to be true. You also know that your gut instincts will never steer you wrong. So, call your energy back, ground, and allow yourself to listen to your gut and take the action that is required. Step out onto your path of destiny, embrace your true divine self, and trust all will work out the way it's meant to be. Trust and believe in yourself.

Affirmation: *I trust and believe in myself, and I follow my gut instinct*

331. PIG – *You Deserve it*

I have come to you today to ask, are you seeing lack around you?

You're looking around you and all you see is what you don't have, what you lack. You're moaning about not having this and that, and you're holding yourself in this energy of lack. Stop, open your eyes, and see all you do have – your home, car, job, business, family, friends, holiday, etc. – and feel gratitude for it all.

The more we get caught up in the energy of lack, the more we attract. So, stop looking at the negative, and start practicing gratitude. Start putting your energy into the gratitude and see how life will change; those things you wanted when you were in the energy of lack will become a reality. Energy flows where your attention goes, so put your energy into gratitude.

Affirmation: *I let go of lack and I embrace the abundance around me now.*

332. HEN – *Explore Further*

I have come to you today to say it's time to explore further.

You have had this nagging feeling that there is something not quite right at the moment with a member of your family or a friend. You just can't seem to put your finger on it. Their behaviour is off, and you know deep down that they are hiding something from you. It's time to explore this feeling you have further. You can do this by asking them about it and letting them know that you're there if they need to talk or need your help.

You can reassure them that you're there to help and guide them if they have a problem, and tell them that everything will work out in the end. It might take time for them to come to you and let you know what is going on, but just let them know that you're there when they need you, and then wait. They will come, you will be able to help them, and all will be OK in the end. Always trust your gut when you get this feeling – it never lets you down.

Affirmation: *I trust my gut instinct always.*

333. PEACOCK – *Pride*

I have come to you today to tell you to walk away with your pride intact.

You're in a situation at the moment that is not very pleasant, and you're finding it hard to keep your pride intact. You feel like screaming and shouting, letting this person have a piece of your mind. You don't normally react like this; you usually let it go over your head. This time is different, you just can't take any more of it, and you're at the end of your tether with it all.

It's not the first time they have treated you like this; you're not going to take it from them anymore. Do a meditation and cut the cords between you, call in Archangel Michael to help you with it, and take back your power from them. Cut all ties with them in the physical and walk away with your pride intact, as they are never going to change – you know this, deep down.

Affirmation: *I walk away with my pride intact now.*

334. DOLPHIN – *Element of Water*

I have come to you today to say you have a very strong connection with the element of water. It pulls you to it and you feel the water within you. It's speaking to you, but you're not aware of this. When you stand beside the water, you feel oneness, and you then go into a meditative state. You have the ability to channel the water for healing and guidance.

The more you connect to the water, the stronger this gift will grow; you must trust and believe in yourself and allow this connection to grow its full potential as you the water has so much wisdom and healing to share with you. You're a natural water keeper – you hold the codes within you. Now is the time to unleash this fully and allow the water to lead you to your destiny and along your soul's path.

Affirmation: *I allow myself to unlock my full potential by connecting with the element of water now.*

335. WHALE – *Find Your True Voice*

I have come to you today to say it's time you found your true voice.

You do speak your truth to some degree, but there is so much more wisdom within. You have been on this path for a long time, and you have done a lot of inner work. You have walked your path, your spiritual journey, but just when you thought that there was no more, there is.

Call on me, the whale, and we can journey together to the depths of your soul and unlock the true wisdom that needs to be spoken. This is your journey to speak your truth and allow others to hear what they need to hear. As you're allowing others to ask questions of themselves, this will bring them back to their true divine selves. Now is your time to unlock that wisdom and free the trapped souls.

Affirmation: *I unlock my wisdom and speak my divine truth now.*

336. SHARK – *Full Potential*

I have come to you today to tell you to stop letting others hold you back from your full potential.

You're allowing others to hold you back, and they are keeping you small. Sometimes you're aware of it, and other times you're not. Feel into the energy and find the reason behind this. Ask yourself what they will gain from holding you back. Are they the right person for you to be around? You can't keep letting them overshadow you like this; this is your time to fly.

You have so much potential, but you can't see it as you're caught up by this other person who is holding you back. Break free from them and allow yourself to fly high; you have so much to offer the world and so many people to help.

Affirmation: *I have unlimited potential.*

335. WHALE – *Find Your True Voice*

I have come to you today to say it's time you found your true voice.

You do speak your truth to some degree, but there is so much more wisdom within. You have been on this path for a long time, and you have done a lot of inner work. You have walked your path, your spiritual journey, but just when you thought that there was no more, there is.

Call on me, the whale, and we can journey together to the depths of your soul and unlock the true wisdom that needs to be spoken. This is your journey to speak your truth and allow others to hear what they need to hear. As you're allowing others to ask questions of themselves, this will bring them back to their true divine selves. Now is your time to unlock that wisdom and free the trapped souls.

Affirmation: *I unlock my wisdom and speak my divine truth now.*

336. SHARK – *Full Potential*

I have come to you today to tell you to stop letting others hold you back from your full potential.

You're allowing others to hold you back, and they are keeping you small. Sometimes you're aware of it, and other times you're not. Feel into the energy and find the reason behind this. Ask yourself what they will gain from holding you back. Are they the right person for you to be around? You can't keep letting them overshadow you like this; this is your time to fly.

You have so much potential, but you can't see it as you're caught up by this other person who is holding you back. Break free from them and allow yourself to fly high; you have so much to offer the world and so many people to help.

Affirmation: *I have unlimited potential.*

337. OCTOPUS – *Open Mind*

I have come to you today to say you must keep an open mind.

You can be quite closed-minded, and you only see what you want to see; this can cause you a bit of bother at times. You're going to encounter a situation where you're going to have to keep an open mind – if you don't, you're going to find it hard to overcome this.

Don't listen to all that you're being told, as some of it's untrue, and this is what's going to cause conflict. You need to look at all aspects of this and be very open-minded. If you do, you will come through this. Don't get caught up other people's drama. Stay in your own lane, make up your own mind, and all will be resolved.

Affirmation: *I stay in my own lane, and I keep an open mind.*

338. SEAHORSE – *Charm*

I have come to you today to say you're a real charmer.

You have a way with people, you always land on your feet no matter what is going on, and nothing seems to bother you. You have a charming effect on people, and you can use this side of you to get what you want – and you do.

It's like luck is always on your side. You let life flow with ease. You don't worry about anything; you don't do stress. When things go wrong, you turn on your charm; you always come out the other side, and you get on with life. This is a great way to be, but others have tried to change you in the past. You do worry sometimes when others criticise you, and it can get you down. It's time that they accept you for you. Don't allow yourself to change for anyone – you are who you are. Let life flow with ease.

Affirmation: *I accept myself for who I am.*

339. GOAT – *Sacrificed*

I have come to you today to ask, is it worth the sacrifice?

You're at a crossroads in life and you can go any way, but you're unsure because one way means you may have to make some sacrifices. Before you make any more moves on which direction you should go, see if the sacrifice is really worth it or not. You're the only one who can answer that.

Sit with it, make a list of the pros and cons, and see which one is better for you in the long run. But be aware that the one that looks the easier option is not always the right one. This decision will affect the rest of your life so don't make it lightly, as you don't want to have any regrets in life. If you're still unsure, ask for guidance, listen very carefully, and then make your decision.

Affirmation: *I allow myself to see the way forward now.*

340. SNAKE – *A Fresh Start*

I have come to you today to say you're being presented with a fresh start.

You have come to a time in your life when you're being presented with a fresh start and you're unclear whether to take it or not. You have been asking for a sign, and this is it. So, yes, make that move to a new home, job, etc. – there is no time like the present, so grip it with both hands.

What are you holding back for? It will all work out, and you will never know until you try, so don't let fear stand in your way. You don't get anywhere in life if you don't take a chance. Take that leap of faith, the universe has your back, and you will look back in a few months' time and ask yourself, 'Why did I make all that fuss?' There is nothing holding you back, so go ahead – take that fresh start and enjoy all that is waiting for you.

Affirmation: *I move forward with ease and grace now.*

341. MONKEY – *Trickster*

I have come to you today to say you have a tricky side to you.

You have a very funny side, and you like to play a trick or two on others and you like to be up to devilment. You find so much joy in having fun, and you don't see how other can be so serious, but you can come across to others as not caring. You just like having fun, playing a few tricks, and that's your way of getting through life.

Yes, sometimes you can go a bit far and get yourself in to trouble. Not everyone sees life the way you do, so the next time you feel like playing a trick on someone, ask yourself how they will react, as this will keep you out of trouble. Keep enjoying life to its fullest; this is the only way you know how to be, so enjoy being you.

Affirmation: *I enjoy life to its fullest.*

342. Gorilla – Overreact

I have come to you today to say you have a tendency to overreact to things going on in life and you make things worse than they actually are. You do this out of fear, then you go into complete overwhelm, and that brings up all sorts of feelings. You can't get yourself back in to balance and everything looks worse than it actually is. The next time you feel you're in a situation, stop, breathe and take it all in before you react. You will be able to deal with the situation at hand.

This will take practice and time, but you will be able to do this. You must keep yourself mindful of what is going on around you and what you're doing. As you do this each time you're in a situation, you will find it easier to deal with it. Before long, it will become natural to you, as the overreacting is just a bad habit which you can change. You will be very aware of it happening and life will get so much easier for you as you bring this into practice.

Affirmation: *I look and assess the situation before I react now.*

343. DEER – *Hectic Life*

I have come to you today to say you're leading a hectic life.

You seem to be always on the move and never staying still for very long. Always looking at what needs to be done next, where to go, etc., but have you ever thought about just sitting still for a few minutes and taking it all in and seeing what is around you? Ask yourself why you're always doing something. Sometimes, we keep ourselves busy as a way of running away from something. It's easier not to look and face our fears sometimes, but we will have to face them eventually. So, why don't you let that time be now?

Take a few days to yourself, clear your schedule, and get to it. It can be hard facing what you have been running away from for years, but surrender to it and just allow what needs to surface. If you're finding it hard, seek help from a mentor, healer, shaman, or whoever you're drawn to. You will get through this, and life can be full of ease and flow, but only if you face your fear and allow it.

Affirmation: *I face my fears now and allow flow and ease into my life.*

344. CAMEL – *Restore and Replenish*

I have come to you today to say it's time for you to take some time off, go and sit in your oasis, and restore and replenish your soul. You must do this before you embark on the next journey of your soul. Allow yourself to do what makes your soul sing, whatever that is – meditate, walk in the forest, sing, dance etc., just allow it to take you where you need to go. You will receive guidance as you do this, so just allow.

Now is your time to nourish yourself on all levels. You have come so far in such a short time, and you must bring in balance. As you come fully into balance, you will gain the strength and guidance that you need to embark on the next part of your soul's journey. Now is your time to restore and replenish your soul. Embrace, enjoy, and allow.

Affirmation: *I restore and replenish my soul now.*

345. GIRAFFE – *Expressing Your Individuality with Pride*

I have come to you today to say, it's time for you to express your individuality with pride.

Stop hiding in the crowd, when you know that is not where you belong. You know you're different from others, so stop trying to fit in. Now is your time to express your individuality, stand out, and allow your true self to shine. You have so much to give to the world, but you can't give and they can't receive if you're hiding.

No more playing it small or hiding behind everyone; you must allow yourself to be seen. You have very unique gifts that can help others along their path, and they are given to you to be used, not hidden. It can be scary when you step out at first, but don't allow others' negativity or fear to hold you back. There are so many people waiting on you to help them, so go ahead and allow your individuality to shine and shine bright with pride. If we were all the same, the world would be a very dull place.

Affirmation: *I allow my Individuality to shine with pride.*

346. SNOW LEOPARD – *Good Karma*

I have come to you today to say it's time for you to attract good karma into your life.

You have done a lot of work on yourself, and you have let go of old patterns, habits, beliefs, and past life and karma patterns, and it has been a challenging time. Now that this is over, it's time to attract good karma into your life.

You can attract good karma into your life by following these five steps daily.

Step 1: Love and forgive yourself; daily affirmations will help you do this.

Step 2: Love and forgive others, let of grudges, and practice forgiveness.

Step 3: Be kind and compassionate to yourself and everyone around you.

Step 4: Reflect, let go of judgement, and gain understanding, not blame.

Step 5: Have patience; this can show you so much.

Follow these steps every day and embrace the good karma in your life.

Affirmation: *I embrace the good karma in my life now.*

347. PANDA – *Integrate*

I have come to you today to say it's time for you to integrate all aspects of yourself.

You have many different aspects of yourself, and you feel scattered at times, but you can't seem to understand why. There are many aspects of you and they see things differently at times, and this can cause inner conflict. Now is the time to call them all back and integrate them into one.

Sit with each aspect of yourself and see what it wants, why it it's behaving the way it is, and do the healing around it. This can be hard as sometimes we don't like what we hear or are afraid of what we might hear, and that's OK. If you can't get to the bottom of it, ask for help from a friend, mentor, or healer, and they will help you along this journey. When you have completed this, you will see the world in a different way.

Affirmation: *I allow and embrace all aspects of myself now.*

348. WORM – *Discover Your Real Strengths*

I have come to you today to say take a look and discover your real strengths.

You feel you have come to a crossroads in life. You have so many tools and gifts that you don't know which direction to go. Stop stressing over it, as that will get you nowhere. Look and see what your real strengths are. See what comes naturally to you; sometimes, when something seems so natural and easy, we don't see it as a strength, and we dismiss it.

You must really look and see what this is, then you can recognise it as your strength. It will all make sense to you when you come to this realisation. Your path will become clear. You have many tools that you can use alongside this, so let go of the worry, allow your path to unfold, and open up to your real strengths. When you're ready, take the next step as it will be waiting for you.

Affirmation: *I recognise my real strengths and I allow my path to unfold now.*

349. HIPPO – Stagnation

I have come to you today to say you have a lot of stagnant energy within you.

You're holding on to stagnant energy, and this is causing you to feel sluggish, with low mood, like you're carrying the weight of the world on your shoulders. Some of it's yours and some belongs to others. You seem to be attracting a lot of drama into your life at the moment, and it's not even yours – this is connected as well.

Go get some healing or do a very deep meditation; after you have done this, you will feel a bit more like yourself. Then you must cleanse and clear your home and workspace and you will start to feel more momentum within your life. You must repeat this once a week for the next four weeks, then every second week, then once a month. This will keep your energy clear, and you will not be picking up other people's stuff.

Affirmation: *I release all stagnant energy from all areas of my life, physical and non-physical, now.*

350. PARROT – *Colours*

I have come to you today to say colours have a huge effect on you.

The colours that you are wearing daily are affecting on you, even down to your mood. Colours have a huge effect on us – they can raise or lower our vibration. We can also use them as a healing tool. Maybe you should look at doing a colour therapy course.

Be mindful of the colours you're wearing and how they are affecting you; also look at the colours in your home and how the mood is in each room and how they are affecting you. You also have a great eye for colours; you just see what matches what, and it's so natural to you. Don't dismiss it, as it's an amazing gift. Start using it to heal yourself, as it's a natural gift of yours. Embrace it and you will see how life can change very quickly when we do what comes naturally to us. No time like the present to put your gifts to work!

Affirmation: *I allow myself to feel and see the vibration of colour now.*

351. MEERKAT – *Gossip*

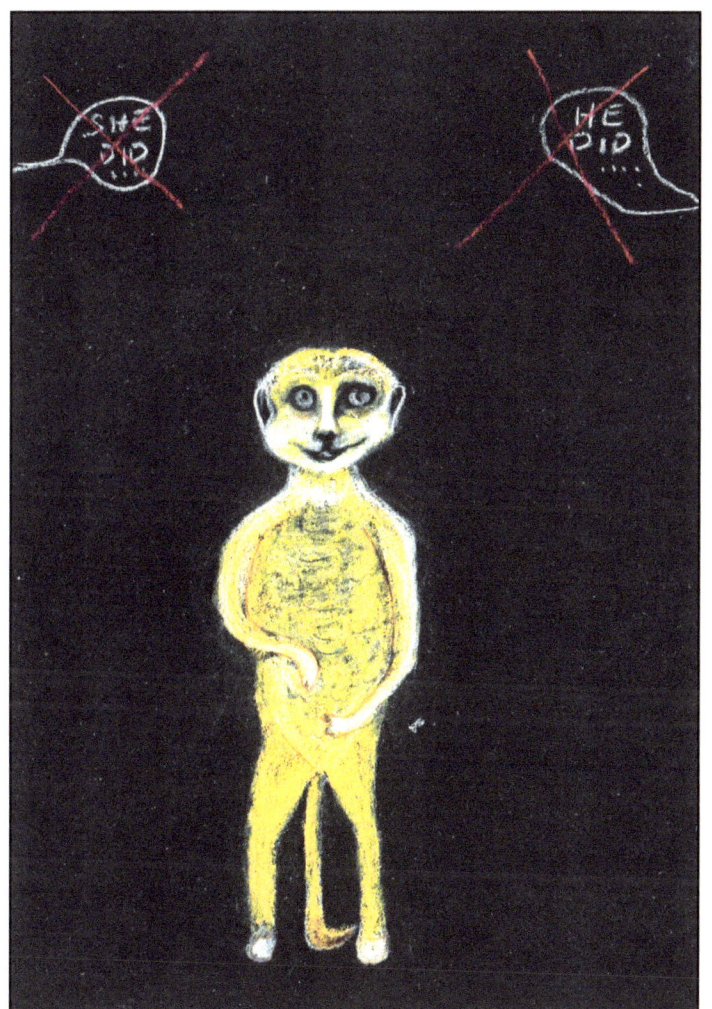

I have come to you today to say don't get caught up in other people's gossip.

We all love to gossip, but you can get caught up in the gossip of others, and it's not good for anyone. When we gossip about others, we are also looking at the things we don't like about ourselves – yes, ourselves.

Gossip is a form of criticism, so why get caught up in it? The next time someone comes to you with gossip, listen and allow, but don't comment or carry it forward; also, see what aspect of it is mirroring you. Look at this aspect, do the clearing and healing around it, and let it go. Then, the next time someone comes to you with gossip, be thankful for what it's showing within you.

Affirmation: *I choose not to gossip.*

352. PANTHER – *Elusive*

I have come to you today to say you have a very elusive personality and a lot of people find it hard to read you. You don't like it when others see the real you. You like that part of your personality, as it keeps a lot of people guessing about you. You don't like people knowing too much about you. You like to do your own thing without looking for others' opinions, and you feel you only have to answer to yourself.

This can be both a good thing and bad thing. When you get it wrong, you don't have anyone to support you, and you find it hard to ask for help. It's OK to let others in and see the real side of you and get the help and support that you need. You might be surprised who will help when asked. You don't have to let everyone in – you can let only the ones you trust the most. When you do, life will change for the better, and you won't feel so alone.

Affirmation: *I allow my guard down now, it's safe.*

353. ZEBRA – *Thinking on Your Feet*

I have come to you today to say you're good at thinking on your feet.

You have a knack when it comes to getting out of any sticky situation, due to your quick-thinking abilities. You have so much confidence with yourself that you don't let anything faze you. You just naturally come up with a solution when you're faced with a tricky situation, and this has helped you out of a lot over the years.

When people ask you how you do it, you say you don't know, as it comes naturally to you –you don't even see what you're doing. You just know what to do or say, and you trust this. Never doubt, just allow, and you will glide through life with ease and flow. Never question it.

Affirmation: *I trust and believe in myself, now and always.*

354. HEDGEHOG – *Emerging Victorious*

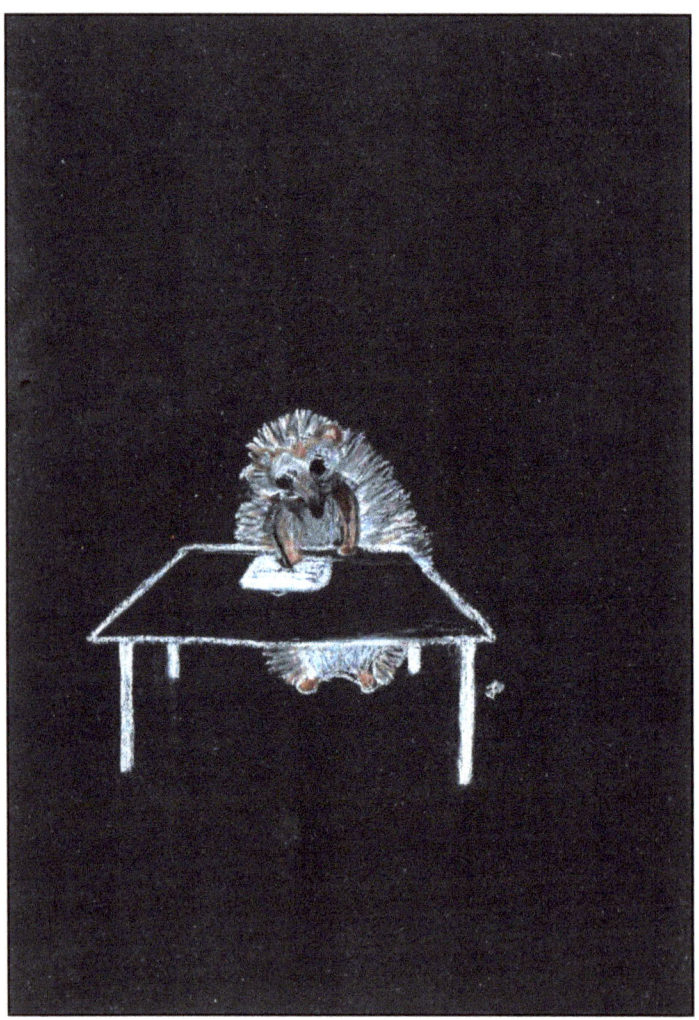

I have come to you today to say you will emerge victorious.

You have been going through a tough time and you're so sick and tired of it. You have been asking for help from everyone you know and your spiritual team; you have done a lot of healing around it, but still no change. You have always relied on someone to help you get out of situations before, but not this time. Your lesson is you will have to figure this one out on your own.

You have all the tools and knowledge that you need. You must look at this situation as an opportunity rather than a problem, which is what you're doing. So, look at it from a different angle and the solution will present itself to you. You're just looking at this in totally the wrong way. Now is your time to take control of your life and not rely on others to sort it out, as you're quite capable of sorting yourself out. There is no lesson in someone else doing it for you, and that's why this lesson keeps occurring. You will sort it out and emerge victorious; believe and trust in yourself.

Affirmation: *I can do anything I put my mind to.*

355. OWL – Graduation

I have come to you today to say you are graduating. (This could also be someone around you.) It's a time for celebration as you or someone around you has reached a milestone in life. It may be a degree, passing an exam, getting a promotion, etc., and now it's time to celebrate. You have worked so hard to get this, and you had so much doubt while doing it and at times felt like giving up. Well done for sticking it out; you have achieved your goal.

The world is your oyster and now is the time to go out and get what you want – there is no stopping you. This achievement will open up a whole new world of opportunity to you. Be very proud of what you have achieved. Now is your time to celebrate, you hard work has paid off.

Affirmation: *The world is my oyster.*

356. BEAR – *Feng Shui*

I have come to you today to tell you to have a look at the old Chinese art of feng shui. You need to bring in the feng shui practice into your home. You just can't seem to get the energy balanced in your home. Start by reading up on this practice and get a better idea of how it can help balance your home. You need to bring in flow, so the energy does not get stagnant in your home.

At the moment, there are a lot of blocks and that is creating stagnant energy, and this affects everyone living there. Your normal clearing will not work. It needs to be done on a deeper level, and that is where the practice of feng shui comes in to create the flow. When you have done this, you will feel the shift in energy in your home, and so will everyone else. Your home will feel balanced, and the energy will flow with ease.

Affirmation: *I bring my home into balance now.*

357. POLAR BEAR – *Emotional Baggage*

I have come to you today to say let go of the old emotional baggage that you're carrying.

Now is the time to let it all go, all that emotional baggage you have been carrying around for years. You have been asking how to surrender and when to do it, and it's time. You have had this heavy burden weighing you down for a long time now. You have been allowing it to affect your decisions, but not anymore – it's time to surrender it now. One way to surrender it is by writing it down on a piece of paper and burning it – it can be that easy if you allow it.

We can make it hard by going into our head and overthinking it and then go into complete overwhelm. That does nobody any good. So, sit down, write it all down, and release it by burning it. You can also imagine a box in front of you and fill it with all the emotions and release it to the universe. You will feel it go when you do this, then thank it for its lesson that you have turned into a blessing. Give yourself permission to release and surrender all that needs to be cleared now.

Affirmation: *I release all emotional baggage now.*

358. SEA LION – *Opportunity Passing You By*

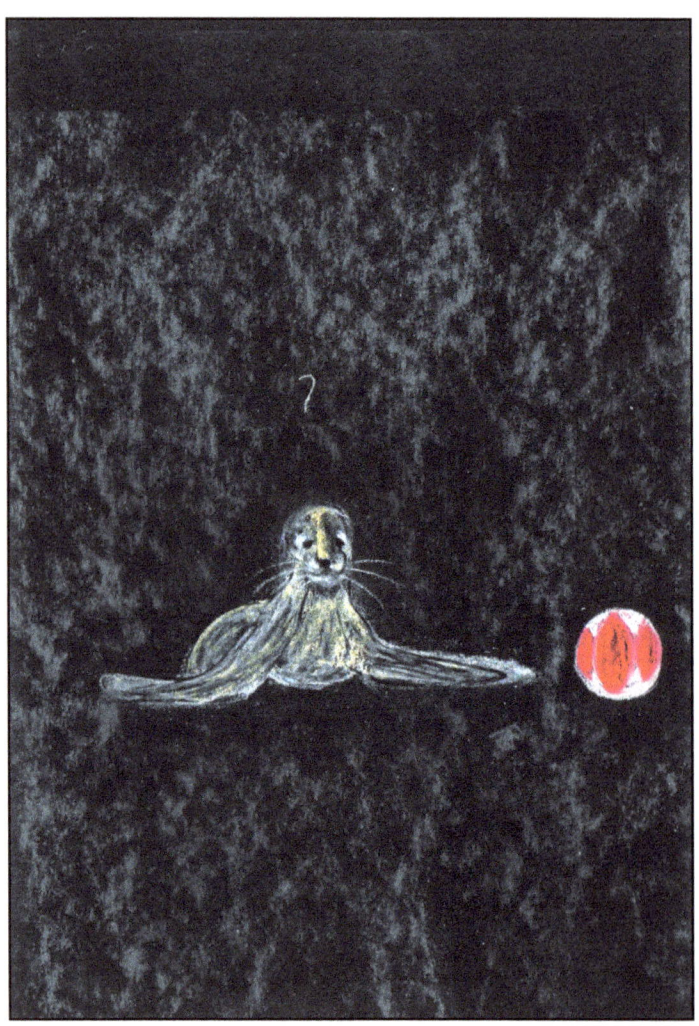

I have come to you today to tell you to open up and see the opportunity passing you by.

You have your sights set on what you don't have, and you're missing the opportunities that are being presented to you. It's like you have a layer of fog around you and you can't see a thing. You have taken your eye off the ball and you're focusing on what you feel you lack and getting caught up in 'poor me'.

This is not like you, so shake off the fog, open your eyes, and see what you have; you have a lot more than most, so stop. Now is the time to see clearly what opportunities are been presented to you and grab them with both hands as they will not be presented to you again. Allow yourself to walk through the door to new beginnings – it's wide open, are you ready to walk through it?

Affirmation: *I clearly see the door of opportunity open before me now.*

359. ANTELOPE – *Knowing Yourself*

I have come to you today to ask, do you really know yourself?

Well, do you? Are there hidden wonders to you? Is there more wisdom to be unearthed? Are you happy the way you are? As a spiritual being, you're always looking to see what next needs to be unearthed within. This is one of those times; you have wisdom within that needs to be unearthed from a past life, and it will help you in this one.

You know there is something deeper within, but you just can't seem to get it. Now is the time to get help from a mentor, shaman, or healer to help release this. You will unearth this wisdom, and it will help you on your soul's path. You will stand fully in your power and speak your truth. You will get to know who you truly are.

Affirmation: *I unlock my true divine self now.*

360. CHAMELEON – *Environment*

I have come to you today to say your environment is affecting your mood.

Somewhere you live, work, or play is affecting your mood. You have noticed every time you go to a certain place, you come out of it with very low energy and it's affecting you quite bad. It can be that there are a lot of spirits or ley lines that are draining your energy, as your light is so bright. Don't panic, this can happen – you just need to protect yourself.

The next time you go to this place, be mindful of how and where your energy is being affected. Wear a crystal for protection, and clear and cleanse your energy. Also, if you know the person in charge of the space well, you can always ask them to do a deep clearing on their space, as it will help them as well as you. You should clear and cleanse your energy at least once a week anyway, as this will keep your energy clear and high. Don't forget to call your energy back as you do this.

Affirmation: *I keep my energy cleansed and clear at all times.*

361. SLOTH – *Avoidance*

I have come to you today to ask, what are you avoiding?

You have been wanting change for some time now; this is the time for that change, but you cannot change unless you go deep within and face what you have been avoiding for some time now. You know deep down that you can't go any further without doing this. Now is that time.

Nobody said this was going to be easy. You can do this, and you will come out the other end. It's going to take time to break this habit down; every time it has come up to be healed and released, you have pushed it down. There are many layers to this, and it will be like peeling them back – each time you clear one, there will be another one waiting for you. You will clear it, but you may need some help to do the deep ones; you will know who to go to get this help. Don't worry, it will be worth it in the end. You will be a much stronger person at the end of it. Just keep telling yourself when things get hard that this too shall end. The change you want is waiting at the other end of this. Have trust and belief in yourself, and be gentle with yourself as you go through this. It will be worth it in the end.

Affirmation: *I peel back the layers, and heal and release what I need to now.*

362. DUCK – *Be Ready, Be Prepared*

I have come to you today to say be ready and be prepared for your life to change unexpectedly. These changes are going to bring you to new heights. You must keep yourself grounded and your head clear at all times, as it's easy to get carried away with it all.

You must stay in your own lane and allow it to unfold naturally. Your wishes are about to manifest, but you must not get carried away. If you do, you will not get fully what you want. It will happen in stages, as you will not be ready for it all at once, so keep your head clear and feet on the ground at all times. Allow, trust, and believe in yourself and always follow your gut, no matter what, as it will never let you down. Most of all, enjoy!

Affirmation: *I am ready and prepared for my wishes to be fulfilled now.*

363. DONKEY – *Extremely Cautious*

I have come to you today to say you must be extremely cautious as you move forward along your path.

You're always in a hurry and you want it now. When you do things, you want to get to the end and move on faster than you should. You glance at things, and you don't always take in everything; this is a habit of yours. You don't sit in the energy long enough to soak it all up, and you want to go to the next stage as quickly as possible – but not this time.

You're about to embark on the next part of your soul's journey and you must have patience as you go along this path; if you don't, you will have to keep redoing it until you take it all in. You must also be extremely cautious not to miss out the key elements of this; they will be given to you as pieces of a puzzle, and you will have to work it out for yourself. So, be cautious you don't miss anything. If you feel yourself falling into your old ways, step back and re-centre. You got this – trust and believe in yourself and all will work out fine.

Affirmation: *I am aware of what I must do now to step forward along my soul's path.*

364. CRAB – *Sideways*

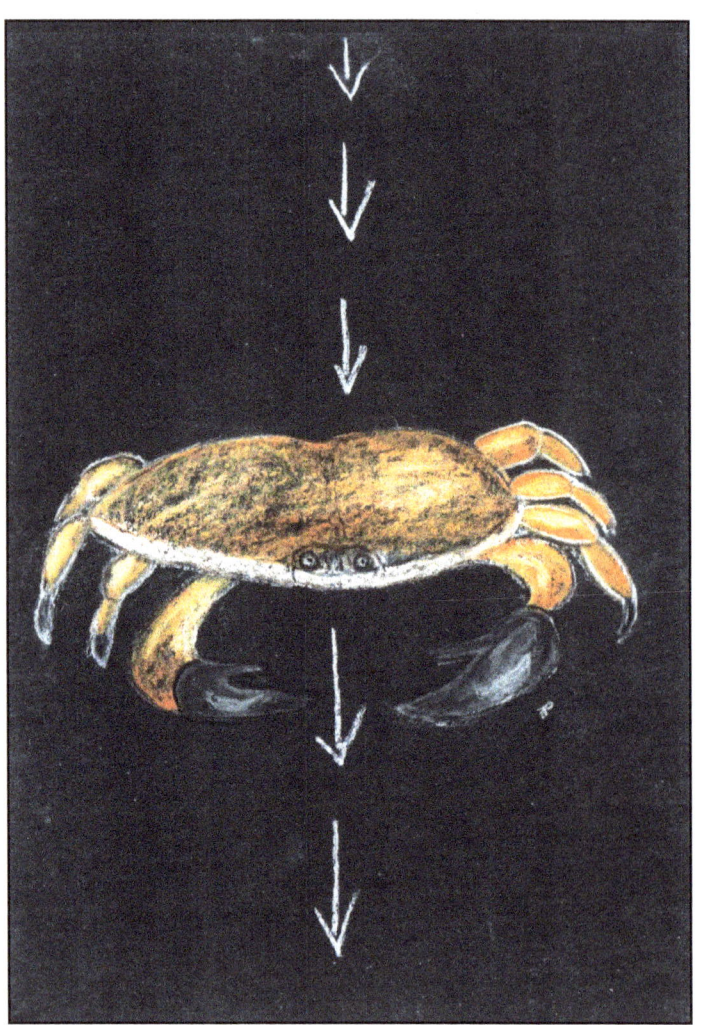

I have come to you today to say stop going backward or sideways.

You have been doing this for a while now; you just can't seem to take the necessary steps forward. This is holding you back on your spiritual journey. When you see something new, you throw yourself head-on into it then discover that it was not meant for you, or you already know it. You then feel like you have stepped backwards or sideways, never forward. You're jumping into everything and anything and not really looking into what you're doing properly.

Now is the time to ask yourself what direction you want to go and what will bring you closer to your soul's path. You know deep down what you want, where to go, and how to get there, but you're just afraid to say it out loud, as you feel others will criticise you for it. That's their problem, not yours, so let them. Now is your time to get clear and take the necessary steps forward – no more sideways or backwards, just forward. So, what are you waiting for? Now is the time to step forward!

Affirmation: *The only steps I take from now on are forward.*

365. BEE – *Trust in the Miracles*

I have come to you today to say it is time for you to trust in the miracles. Yes, trust in the miracles, they do happen; all you need is faith. You have been asking for a miracle of late and your faith is wavering. You're the end of your tether at this moment in time, and you just can't see any end to it. Hang on in there, it will happen, so hold onto your faith.

It cannot happen until everything is in full alignment and what needs to be done is done. Your guides are working away in the background, you just can't see. So, hang on a little bit longer; it's all going to change for the better. Things will start to align in your favour; people, places, and situations will start to appear, and then the change you want will happen. That new beginning is on the horizon for you.

Affirmation: *I hold onto my faith, and I am open to all possibilities now.*

Acknowledgments

I would like to thank my husband, Bernard, for all the love, support and encouragement you have given while I was writing this book and beyond.

Thank you to my two sons, Eirnín and Ciarán, for being who you are; I love you with all my heart.

My dear friends Caroline, Fergie, Hannah, Jack, Finn, and Ellie for always being there for me, no matter what. For the endless cups of tea, love and laughter. You're the friends I choose as my family.

My two brothers, Fabian and Paul, and their families: thank you for the laughter and tears over the years, even at times I know you were thinking that your sister had lost her mind, and for fully accepting me for who I am, madness and all.

My childhood friend Tracey who has helped through so much over the past 40 years plus: thank you for being you.

My Soul Sister Deirdre, whom I met at the start of my journey, who has been with me through every major breakthrough: when the self-doubt kicked in, you always had the words to help me push through it. Thank you for being you.

My Soul Sister Orla: you came into my life a few years ago and you have had a major impact on it. Thank you for being you.

My Soul Sister Yvonne: for healings, tea, laughter, and the nuttiness we have on a weekly basis. Thank you for being you.

My Soul Sister Lisa: for all your words of encouragement always.

Marcia O'Regan, my mentor and Soul Sister: for all your help over the years, for always believing in me, for pushing me to the next level; you have truly helped me get where I am today. You have never walked in front of me or behind me – you have always walked beside me. You're a true blessing in my life. Thank you for being you.

Aishling Money, my first spiritual mentor: without you helping me see and embrace the spirit animal guides, this book would not have been possible.

Jenny Parris: thank you for bringing each guidance in this book to life with your amazing illustrations; this book would not be complete without you.

Fiona: For the endless cups of tea and chats, thank you for being you.

To all the healers, therapists, coaches and workshops I have done work with over the years: each one of you played your part in getting me to this point on my soul's journey. Thank you from the bottom of my heart.

To all my clients over the years, who trusted me and my guides: thank you for allowing me to do the work that I love so much, helping you along your soul's journey.

To everyone who has crossed my path along my soul's journey: Thank you.

About the Author

Sharon Brown is a mother, wife, animal lover, high vibrational healer, spirit animal intuitive, and galactic master. Over the years, Sharon has studied many healing modalities – mediumship and shamanism, to name a couple.

Sharon lives in a small village in North County, Dublin. She is passionate about animals and holds a soft spot for dogs. Meeting up with her friends brings so much joy into her life, and she loves nothing better than being in the middle of a forest, connecting with the elementals, as this makes her soul sing.

Sharon is a soul connector who realigns her clients back to the essence of who they truly are, at their highest vibration of source to help them rediscover their purpose and their truest life path.

Website: https://sharonbrown.net/

Facebook: https://www.facebook.com/livinguniquelyusharon.ie

Instagram: https://www.instagram.com/sharonbrownthesoulconnector/

About the Artist

I am Jenny Parris and as a natural healer, I have found myself training in many modalities.

It was whilst attending an angel retreat a few years ago that Sharon and I met, when she led the group to meet their own particular spirit animal.

I was honoured to be asked to do the illustrations for Sharon's book, and by linking in with each animal and channelled message, I was able to bring forward the pictures – many of which made me laugh out loud at the picture I was seeing in my mind.

I also work with angels, the Inner Child, and a channelled tool called Enlighten the Shadow Within.

I live in Cornwall with my partner and love to connect to the beauty of Mother Nature and all that she holds.

Website: http://www.artistichealing.net/

www.ingramcontent.com/pod-product-compliance
Lightning Source LLC
Chambersburg PA
CBHW042357280426
43661CB00096B/1140